Men in the Off Hours

Men in the Off Hours

....

ANNE CARSON

....

Alfred A. Knopf : *New York*

2 0 0 0

THIS IS A BORZOI BOOK

PUBLISHED BY ALFRED A. KNOPF

Copyright © 2000 by Anne Carson

www.randomhouse.com

Some of the poems in this collection were originally published in the following:
American Poetry Review: "Catullus: *Carmina*"; *Chicago Review:* "Shadowboxer"; *Conjunctions:*
"TV Men: Artaud"; *Fence:* "Ordinary Time: Virginia Woolf and Thucydides on War" and "Appen-
dix to Ordinary Time"; *The New Yorker:* "New Rule" and "Father's Old Blue Cardigan"; *Paris
Review:* "Flatman" and "TV Men: Antigone"; *Parnassus:* "TV Men: Lazarus"; *PN Review:* "TV
Men: Akhmatova"; *Raritan:* "Essay on What I Think About Most," "Hopper: *Confessions*" and
"TV Men: Tolstoy"; *Seneca Review:* "Irony Is Not Enough: Essay on My Life as Catherine
Deneuve"; *The Threepenny Review:* "Epitaph: Oedipus' Nap" and "TV Men: Thucydides in
Conversation with Virginia Woolf on the Set of *The Peloponnesian War*"; *Princeton University
Press, Before Sexuality* (1990), edited by F. Zeitlin and D. Halperin: "Dirt and Desire: Essay on the
Phenomenology of Female Pollution in Antiquity."

ISBN 0-375-40803-7

Manufactured in the United States of America
Published March 3, 2000
Second Printing, April 2000

CONTENTS

....

Men in the Off Hours

ORDINARY TIME: VIRGINIA WOOLF AND THUCYDIDES ON WAR

I like the way Thucydides begins his account of the hostilities between Athenians and Peloponnesians that we call the Peloponnesian War. The account begins Book 2 of his *History.* For he has spent Book I telling what happened before the beginning, which he calls "archaeology." His archaeology reads like a swirling dust of anecdotes and speech and usual pretexts and true causes. His beginning, on the other hand, is sharp. He names seven different ways of telling time:

> The thirty years' truce which had been concluded
> after the capture of Euboea remained unbroken
> for 14 years; but in the 15th year, when Chrysis
> was in the 48th year of her priesthood at Argos,
> and Ainesias was ephor at Sparta, and Pythodoros
> had still 4 months to serve as archon at Athens,
> in the 16th month after the battle of Potidaea,
> at the opening of spring, some Thebans, a little more
> than 300 in number, entered under arms into Plataea
> about the first watch of the night. . . .
>
> (2.2.1)

Thucydides fixes the commencement of the war according to the forms of reckoning customary in the three most important Hellenic states; we learn how they tell time in Argos and Sparta and Athens. How people tell time is an intimate and local fact about them. Thucydides sets us on a high vantage point above such facts, so that we look down as if at a map of the Greek states and see lives churning forward there—each in

....

its own time zone, its own system of measures, its own local names. Soon this manifold will fuse into one time and system, under the name of war. But first we see it as hard separate facts.

Then we see separateness caught in a larger necessity. For the local time zones of Argos, Sparta and Athens are framed by reference to the capture of Euboea and the battle of Potidaea, two historical events detailed by Thucydides himself in Book I of his *History.* A historian's account will necessarily encompass local ways of telling time. Still, even this is not final.

Historiographical time is itself bound by the habits of nature. Thucydides decided military history should be dated as to campaigning seasons. "The events of the war have been recorded in the order of their occurrence, summer by summer and winter by winter," he says at the beginning of Book II (2.1.1). Naturally he locates the affair of the Thebans who entered Plataea, which triggered the war and so came just before the first summer, "at the opening of spring . . ." (2.1.2).

And perhaps because he himself did not sleep well—for he wrote his *History* from exile, having been banished in 424 B.C. for failing to prevent the reduction of Amphipolis, and may have stayed awake for twenty years somewhere in Thrace or the Peloponnese, following the war with close attention by day and writing up his notes at night—he marks the start of that long interval: "about the first watch of the night. . . ."

Virginia Woolf wrote "The Mark on the Wall" at the start of the First World War. She too begins with chronology. But she does not, like Thucydides, rise above ordinary time to a high point and look down on other people, other people's reckonings. She stays in her own time. She stays right in the middle. "It was in the middle of January in the present year when I . . ." But how do you know what is the middle? As time it is vague. Its borders reach to the edges of what one saw from where one sat. What one saw was fire, yellow light on pages, chrysanthemums in a round glass bowl, cigarette smoke, burning coals, an old fancy of crimson flags and red knights riding up the black rock. What one saw was the middle of time. One saw nothing happening there, for nothing ever happens there. Until it does. "To my relief the sight of the mark interrupted. . . ."

For Virginia Woolf, as for Thucydides, it is important to mark the beginning of war. Otherwise, and so easily, it will lose itself into the middle of time . . . "always the most mysterious of losses." No photographs of ruined houses or dead bodies are yet in evidence in 1914. And Thucydides tells us the Thebans entered Plataea "because they foresaw war coming and wished to get Plataea while there was still peace, war being not yet obvious" (2.2.3). Indeed, little was obvious that night. The Thebans slipped into Plataea unobserved, by intrigue of some partisans within the town, then at once lost track of their own strategy. Their plan had been clear: to attack immediately. Instead they grounded their arms in the marketplace, sat down, and proclaimed a negotiation. Why? It was the beginning of their death. Thucydides offers no explanation—"what an accidental affair this living is after all our civilization," says Virginia Woolf. Meanwhile the Plataeans were dismantling their civilization from the inside—digging through the party walls between their houses in order to gather and sally forth in strength against the Thebans. They waited for the blackness before dawn.

They attacked.

"With one's hair flying back like the tail of a race horse," says Virginia Woolf of the rapidity of life. Death too is rapid—in panic streets on a moonless night ("for these things took place at the end of the month," Thucydides notes [2.4.2]) and it was raining, not just rain but stones and ceramic tiles from women and slaves who stood on the roofs and pelted the Thebans, screaming. They died because in the black substance of someone else's night all the streets looked the same . . . "all so casual, all so haphazard. . . ." All the trees looked like men. Someone barred the gate where they had come in, not with a proper door pin but the spike of a javelin: no rules to go by anymore! And perhaps it was from this they suddenly knew, as they ran slipping in mud, that peace was over and war was on. For peace is a matter of generalizations. "Sunday afternoon walks, Sunday luncheons, and also ways of speaking of the dead, clothes and habits—like the habit of sitting all together in a room until a certain hour although nobody liked it. There was a rule for everything." Whereas in war—"shot out at the feet of God entirely naked!" she says and he describes the naked Thebans taken alive in a room at the end of a street. Whether or not they were *hostages* in a technical sense is unclear. Certainly Thebes negotiated with Plataea for their lives in good faith and afterward alleged that the Plataeans promised on oath to restore them (2.5.5). Plataea denies an oath was sworn (2.5.6). "Once a thing's done, no one ever knows how it happened," she says. "There will be nothing but spaces of light and dark." Was it a space of light or of dark where all those who had been taken captive were slain, 180 in number, including Eurymachos with whom the partisans had originally treated, so that the herald on his arrival found not a stalk upright.

At the beginning of war, when rules and time and freedom are just starting to slip off the lines, you can sit and think quietly about a mark on the wall. Is it black, is it a hole, made by a nail or some round substance, in certain lights does it not seem actually to project from the wall, "to cast a perceptible shadow"? Speculation is "agreeably philosophic," she says and compares herself to a retired colonel speculating about some small mounds on the South Downs. Are they tombs or camps? Does it matter? Once war gets going, most camps will be tombs soon enough. Thucydides tells us that war got going right after Plataea:

. . . .

> Nothing paltry in the designs of either side: they
> were strong for war and not without reason.
>
> (2.8.1)

Reason and strength belong to the beginning. "For at the beginning men all take hold more sharply," he says of the Athenians and Peloponnesians as they laid themselves into war (2.8.1). And pursuing his meditation on time—flesh of the world, fed into war, not coming back—he adds:

> Just then, youth—which was abundant in the Peloponnese,
> abundant among the Athenians—youth (due to its inexperience)
> embraced the war.
>
> (2.8.1)

Time embraces youth, youth embraces war. See the circles fit one upon the other. See them move and slip, turning around a center which becomes gradually emptier, gradually darker, until it is as black as a mark on the wall.

Virginia Woolf concludes "The Mark on the Wall" abruptly. Amidst speculation she notices someone standing over her who says: "I'm going out to buy a newspaper."

The odd thing is, and although incidental it may be the reason why she ends the essay this way, you grasp at once without any mention of the fact that someone is a man. He could no more be a woman than Thucydides. Not only because of his need for newspapers and view of the war ("Though it's no good buying newspapers. . . . Nothing ever happens. Curse this war. . . !") but because he at once identifies the mark on the wall as what it is. A snail is a snail. Even in the off hours, men know marks.

....

7

In his *History* Thucydides begins the war "at the opening of spring." After that he notices only campaigning seasons: ordinary time is marked "by summers and winters." Spring disappears. So it was winter, less than twelve months after the incident at Plataea, when the Athenians, using a custom of their fathers, gave burial at public expense to those who had fallen in the first year of the war. Over them Pericles pronounced a funeral oration, wherein he is said to have remarked that the vanishing of young men from the country was as if the spring were taken out of the year (Aristotle, *Rhetoric*, 1411a3; cf. 1365a32). "There is a vast upheaval of matter," says Virginia Woolf just before she notices someone standing over her. And in a letter (written some years later) she recalls the moment:

> I shall never forget the day I wrote "The Mark on the Wall"—all in a flash, as if flying, after being kept stone breaking for months . . . and then Leonard came in and I drank my milk and concealed my excitement.
>
> (letter to Ethel Smyth, 16 October 1930)

EPITAPH: ZION

Murderous little world once our objects had gazes. Our lives
       Were fragile, the wind
Could dash them away. Here lies the refugee breather
       Who drank a bowl of elsewhere.

FIRST CHALDAIC ORACLE

There is something you should know.
And the right way to know it
is by a cherrying of your mind.

Because if you press your mind towards it
and try to know
that thing

as you know a thing,
you will not know it.
It comes out of red

with kills on both sides,
it is scrap, it is nightly,
it kings your mind.

No. Scorch is not the way
to know
that thing you must know.

But use the hum
of your wound
and flamepit out everything

right to the edge
of that thing you should know.
The way to know it

....

is not by staring hard.
But keep chiselled
keep Praguing the eye

of your soul and reach—
mind empty
towards that thing you should know

until you get it.
That thing you should know.
Because it is out there (orchid) outside your *and*, it is.

NEW RULE

A New Year's white morning of hard new ice.
High on the frozen branches I saw a squirrel jump and skid.
Is this scary? he seemed to say and glanced

down at me, clutching his branch as it bobbed
in stiff recoil—or is it just that everything sounds wrong today?
The branches

clinked.
He wiped his small cold lips with one hand.
Do you fear the same things as

I fear? I countered, looking up.
His empire of branches slid against the air.
The night of hooks?

The man blade left open on the stair?
Not enough spin on it, said my true love
when he left in our fifth year.

The squirrel bounced down a branch
and caught a peg of tears.
The way to hold on is

afterwords
so
clear.

. . . .

SUMPTUOUS DESTITUTION

"Sumptuous destitution"

Your opinion gives me a serious feeling: I would like to be what you deem me.

> (Emily Dickinson letter 319 to Thomas Higginson)

is a phrase

You see my position is benighted.

> (Emily Dickinson letter 268 to Thomas Higginson)

scholars use

She was much too enigmatical a being for me to solve in an hour's interview.

> (Thomas Higginson letter 342a to Emily Dickinson)

of female

God made me [Sir] Master—I didn't be—myself.

> (Emily Dickinson letter 233 to Thomas Higginson)

silence.

Rushing among my small heart—and pushing aside the blood—

> (Emily Dickinson letter 248 to Thomas Higginson)

Save what you can, Emily.

And when I try to organize—my little Force explodes—and leaves me bare and charred. (Emily Dickinson letter 271 to Thomas Higginson)

Save every bit of thread.

Have you a little chest to put the Alive in?

> (Emily Dickinson letter 233 to Thomas Higginson)

One of them may be

By Cock, said Ophelia.

> (Emily Dickinson letter 268 to Thomas Higginson)

the way out of here.

....

EPITAPH: ANNUNCIATION

Motion swept the world aside, aghast to white nerve nets.
      Pray what
Shall I do with my six hundred wings? as a blush feels
      Slow, from inside.

HOKUSAI

Anger is a bitter lock.
But you can turn it.

Hokusai aged 83
said,
Time to do my lions.

Every morning
until he died

219 days later
he made
a lion.

Wind came gusting from the northwest.

Lions swayed
and leapt
from the crests

of the pine trees
onto

the snowy road
or crashed
together

....

over his hut,
their white paws

mauling stars
on the way down.

I continue to draw
hoping for
a peaceful day,

said Hokusai
as they thudded past.

AUDUBON

Audubon perfected a new way of drawing birds that he called his.
On the bottom of each watercolor he put "drawn from nature"
which meant he shot the birds

and took them home to stuff and paint them.
Because he hated the unvarying shapes
of traditional taxidermy

he built flexible armatures of bent wire and wood
on which he arranged bird skin and feathers—
or sometimes

whole eviscerated birds—
in animated poses.
Not only his wiring but his lighting was new.

Audubon colors dive in through your retina
like a searchlight
roving shadowlessly up and down the brain

until you turn away.
And you do turn away.
There is nothing to see.

You can look at these true shapes all day and not see the bird.
Audubon understands light as an absence of darkness,
truth as an absence of unknowing.

. . . .

It is the opposite of a peaceful day in Hokusai.
Imagine if Hokusai had shot and wired 219 lions
and then forbade his brush to paint shadow.

"We are what we make ourselves," Audubon told his wife
when they were courting.
In the salons of Paris and Edinburgh

where he went to sell his new style
this Haitian-born Frenchman
lit himself

as a noble rustic American
wired in the cloudless poses of the Great Naturalist.
They loved him

for the "frenzy and ecstasy"
of true American facts, especially
in the second (more affordable) octavo edition (*Birds of America*, 1844).

EPITAPH: EUROPE

Once live X-rays stalked the hills as if they were
       Trees. Bones stay now
And their Lent stays with them, black on the nail.
       Tattering on the daywall.

FREUD (1st draft)

Freud spent the summer of 1876 in Trieste

researching hermaphroditism in eels.

In the lab of zoologist Karl Klaus

he dissected

more than a thousand to check whether they had testicles.

"All the eels I have cut open are of the tenderer sex,"

he reported after the first 400.

Meanwhile

the "young goddesses" of Trieste were proving

unapproachable.

"Since

it is not permitted

to dissect human beings I have

in fact nothing to do with them," he confided in a letter.

LAZARUS (1st draft)

Inside the rock on which we live, another rock.

So they believe.

What is a Lamb of God? People use this phrase.

I don't know.

I watch my sister, fingers straying absently about her mustache,

no help there.

Leaves stir through the house like souls, they stream

from the porch,

catch in the speaking holes, glow and are gone.

Remember

what Prince Andrei said when they told him Moscow had burnt

right down to the ground.

He said *Really?*

A man who had been to the war! had seen our lives are just blind arrows

flying.

There he sat

on his cot all the same, trying to get the string to the bowhorn.

Actions go on in us,

nothing else goes on. While a blurred and breathless hour

repeats, repeats.

FLATMAN (1st draft)

I was born in the circus. I play the flat man.
      My voice is flat, my walk is flat, my ironies
            move flatly out to sock you in the eye.

Hands, feet, vowels, hair, shadow, feelings of community,
      strings (you do not see) all flat.
            The epic model I guess I'll

pass over, Homer likening stalemate in war to a carpenter's
      chalkline. My flat world cost only $2 to view
            at first, later this price like others went up.

Brute natures and angels in transparent draperies all alike
      enjoyed the show. Flowers fell
            transparently off them as they entered my tent

where air was of course planar. In some other world they
      could have stayed organized but something about me
            cast their placards down (flat yes):

Brechtian. See a flat rat escape that one-dimensional skull.
      And then, and then, what whispers there.
            Your agony, mine, in the fully consensual design

of this play of light—you crowd of missing ones,
      return the ball to me! whispers, whispers and her voice
            (she never arrives) froze on the knock.

Flat thunder, all my heart, you might use Brahms behind it.
      Dull, whitish, deadly as a carpenter's chalkline.
            Not Beethoven—Beethoven I cannot flatten.

....

A STATION

I was reading a life of George Eliot.
After marrying Cross
she caught laryngitis
and three pages later lay in the grave.
"The grave was deep and narrow."
Why so sad, I hardly knew her.
Saddest of all the little dropped comments.
Someone passing Highgate:
Is it the late George Eliot's wife going to be buried?
Up the hill and through the rain by a road unknown
to Hampstead and a station.

EPITAPH: DONNE CLOWN

Tho' perfect joint of moon I doe commend me to you.
      Because of the kind of death it was,
Finger on your lippe. Doe foxes need axes?
      No, coldlights. Eye at all.

FLAT MAN (2nd draft)

If you see this card half out of my pocket you know
I am in on the bidding.
Don't wait to feel it
on the pulse: I was

evacuated May Day from an explosive island
where I had made my home.
Sulfur dioxide thick in the air,
microgravity readings worrisome,

twilight hard to distinguish from other times of day—
I had got blasé about the ash cloud when
fiery hail began hitting the pool.
Suddenly it was night in the kitchen.

As I am now at hand with my card in my pocket
you know I did not put God in my debt that day.
Here is the thing though:
I do not organize well anymore.

"My little Force . . ." as Emily said.
Barest panoramics imply internal difference
Where the Mountains Are.
Or were.

But
be assured my shamefastness,
though pungent, is complete.
And I can pay.

. . . .

EPITAPH: OEDIPUS' NAP

Scorched to wake lawless, loose
     In the sockets of him.
A fell dark pink February heaven
     Was
Pulling the clouds home, balancing massacre
     On the rips.

SHADOWBOXER

Of the soldier who put a spear through Christ's side on the cross
(and by some accounts broke his legs),
whose name was Longinus,
it is said
that after that he had trouble sleeping
and fell into a hard mood,
drifted out of the army
and came west,
as far as Provincia.
Was a body's carbon not simply carbon.
Jab hook jab.
Slight shift and we catch him
in a moment of expansion and catastrophe,
white arms sporting strangely in a void.
Uppercut jab jab hook jab.
Don't want to bore you,
my troubles jab.
Jab.
Jab.
Punch hook.
Jab. *Was a face not all stille*
as dew in Aprille.
Hook.
Jab.
Jab.

LAZARUS (2nd draft)

Other bait pushed their way past me with cloaklike flutters.
Whitish clouds puffed from the smoke machine.
It's nontoxic said God.
Nothing is nontoxic.
God laughed.
Dear old red eyes, what did you hope—
Just shove it through the night slot
and let's go.
Free use of one's own being is most difficult,
is it not.
That panting—
I shall,
when shall I not
hear it.

....

EPITAPH: EVIL

To get the sound take everything that is not the sound drop it
       Down a well, listen.
Then drop the sound. Listen to the difference
       Shatter.

ESSAY ON WHAT I THINK ABOUT MOST

Error.

And its emotions.

On the brink of error is a condition of fear.

In the midst of error is a state of folly and defeat.

Realizing you've made an error brings shame and remorse.

Or does it?

Let's look into this.

Lots of people including Aristotle think error

an interesting and valuable mental event.

In his discussion of metaphor in the *Rhetoric*

Aristotle says there are 3 kinds of words.

Strange, ordinary and metaphorical.

"Strange words simply puzzle us;

ordinary words convey what we know already;

it is from metaphor that we can get hold of something new & fresh"

(*Rhetoric*, 1410b10–13).

In what does the freshness of metaphor consist?

Aristotle says that metaphor causes the mind to experience itself

in the act of making a mistake.

He pictures the mind moving along a plane surface

of ordinary language

when suddenly

that surface breaks or complicates.

Unexpectedness emerges.

....

At first it looks odd, contradictory or wrong.
Then it makes sense.
And at this moment, according to Aristotle,
the mind turns to itself and says:
"How true, and yet I mistook it!"
From the true mistakes of metaphor a lesson can be learned.

Not only that things are other than they seem,
and so we mistake them,
but that such mistakenness is valuable.
Hold onto it, Aristotle says,
there is much to be seen and felt here.
Metaphors teach the mind

to enjoy error
and to learn
from the juxtaposition of *what is* and *what is not* the case.
There is a Chinese proverb that says,
Brush cannot write two characters with the same stroke.
And yet

that is exactly what a good mistake does.
Here is an example.
It is a fragment of ancient Greek lyric
that contains an error of arithmetic.
The poet does not seem to know
that $2 + 2 = 4$.

. . . .

Alkman fragment 20:

> *[?] made three seasons, summer*
> *and winter and autumn third*
> *and fourth spring when*
> *there is blooming but to eat enough*
> *is not.*

Alkman lived in Sparta in the 7th century B.C.
Now Sparta was a poor country
and it is unlikely
that Alkman led a wealthy or well-fed life there.
This fact forms the background of his remarks
which end in hunger.

Hunger always feels
like a mistake.
Alkman makes us experience this mistake
with him
by an effective use of computational error.
For a poor Spartan poet with nothing

left in his cupboard
at the end of winter—
along comes spring
like an afterthought of the natural economy,
fourth in a series of three,
unbalancing his arithmetic

and enjambing his verse.
Alkman's poem breaks off midway through an iambic metron
with no explanation
of where spring came from
or why numbers don't help us
control reality better.

There are three things I like about Alkman's poem.
First that it is small,
light
and more than perfectly economical.
Second that it seems to suggest colors like pale green
without ever naming them.

Third that it manages to put into play
some major metaphysical questions
(like Who made the world)
without overt analysis.
You notice the verb "made" in the first verse
has no subject: [?]

It is very unusual in Greek
for a verb to have no subject, in fact
it is a grammatical mistake.
Strict philologists will tell you
that this mistake is just an accident of transmission,
that the poem as we have it

....

is surely a fragment broken off
some longer text
and that Alkman almost certainly did
name the agent of creation
in the verses preceding what we have here.
Well that may be so.

But as you know the chief aim of philology
is to reduce all textual delight
to an accident of history.
And I am uneasy with any claim to know exactly
what a poet means to say.
So let's leave the question mark there

at the beginning of the poem
and admire Alkman's courage
in confronting what it brackets.
The fourth thing I like
about Alkman's poem
is the impression it gives

of blurting out the truth in spite of itself.
Many a poet aspires
to this tone of inadvertent lucidity
but few realize it so simply as Alkman.
Of course his simplicity is a fake.
Alkman is not simple at all,

he is a master contriver—
or what Aristotle would call an "imitator"
of reality.
Imitation (*mimesis* in Greek)
is Aristotle's collective term for the true mistakes of poetry.
What I like about this term

is the ease with which it accepts
that what we are engaged in when we do poetry is error,
the willful creation of error,
the deliberate break and complication of mistakes
out of which may arise
unexpectedness.

So a poet like Alkman
sidesteps fear, anxiety, shame, remorse
and all the other silly emotions associated with making mistakes
in order to engage
the fact of the matter.
The fact of the matter for humans is imperfection.

Alkman breaks the rules of arithmetic
and jeopardizes grammar
and messes up the metrical form of his verse
in order to draw us into this fact.
At the end of the poem the fact remains
and Alkman is probably no less hungry.

....

Yet something has changed in the quotient of our expectations.

For in mistaking them,

Alkman has perfected something.

Indeed he has

more than perfected something.

Using a single brushstroke.

ESSAY ON ERROR (2nd draft)

It is also true I dream about soiled suede gloves.

And have done so

since the day I read

in the third published volume of Freud's letters

(this was years after I stopped seeing him)

a sentence which I shall quote here in full.

Letter to Ferenczi 7.5.1909:

"He doesn't look a bit like a poet except for the lashes."

Freud hesitates to name me

but

let me tell you

that was no

pollen stain.

Here

I could paraphrase Descartes

the hand that busy instrument

or just let it go.

After all

what are you and I compared to him?

Smell of burnt pastilles.

I still remember the phrase every time I pass that spot.

....

CATULLUS: *CARMINA*

I LOVE YOU JOHNNY AND I DIDN'T DO ANYTHING

(big white letters chalked on a rock in the Mojave Desert)

Passer Deliciae Meae Puellae (My Lady's Pet)

Catullus observes his love and her pet at play.

On her lap one of the matted terriers.

She was combing around its genitals.

It grinned I grinned back.

It's the one she calls *Little Bottle* after Deng Xiaoping.

Lugete O Veneres Cupidinesque (Mourn O Venuses and Cupids)

Catullus sings a dirge.

Today Death stormed in and took *Little Bottle* and left.

No more little black hooligan clods of earth

Across her white bedspread.

Death makes me think (I said) about soldiers and autumn.

One carries.

One carries.

One carries it.

....

Salve Nec Minimo Puella Naso (Hello Not Very Small Nosed Girl)

Catullus compares an unnamed girl to his own love.

Your nose is wrong.
Your feet are wrong.
Your eyes are wrong your mouth is wrong.
Your pimp is wrong even his name is wrong.
Who cares what they say, you're not—
Why can't I
Live in the nineteenth century.

Iam Ver Egelidos Refert Tepores (Now Spring Brings Warmths)

Catullus greets the season.

Now spring unlocks.
Now the equinox stops its blue rages quiet
As pages.
I tell you leave Troy leave the ground burning, they did.
Look we will change everything all the meanings
All the clear cities of Asia you and me.
Now the mind isn't she an avid previous hobo?
Now the feet grow leaves so glad to see whose green baits.
Awaits.
Oh sweet don't go.
Back the same way go a new way.

....

Hesterno Licini Die Otiosi (Yesterday Licinius at Our Ease)

Catullus addresses Licinius with affection.

I guess around sunset we started to drink.
And lay on the floor writing lines
For songs that cold
Night smell coming in
The window I left about four went
Home.
Opened the fridge.
Closed it lay down got up.
Lay down.
Lay.
Turned.
Not morning yet.
I just want to talk to you.
Why does love happen?
So then I grew old and died and wrote this.
Be careful it's worldsharp.

Caeli Lesbia Nostra Lesbia Illa (Our Lesbia That Lesbia)

Catullus finds his own love gone to others.

Nuns coated in silver were not so naked
As our night interviews.
Now what plum is your tongue
In?

....

Nulli Se Dicit Mulier Mea Nubere Malle (No One She Says)

Catullus wonders about lovers' oaths.

No one but you she says she swore.

Why one night a god threw open the door.

I loved you more.

River.

River.

River.

River.

River.

River.

River.

River   river   river   river   river   river   river.

Huc Est Mens Deducta Tua Mea Lesbia Culpa
                    (To This Point Is My Mind Reduced)

Catullus is brought low.

Decay flaps upward from my mind O my love.

Where it fingers your crime.

The autumn night comes on so cool.

Siqua Recordanti Benefacta Priora Voluptas
(If for a Man Recalling Prior Benefactions)

Catullus reflects on his own piety.

Before my holy stoning in the wet kisses and the smell of sperm
I drove an ambulance for the Red Cross.
Do you think a man can be naturally pure?
In those days I kept a diary it fell out of my pocket the night
I carried you to the forge in my arms.
You grew freer and brighter with every stroke of the hammer.

Odi et Amo (I Hate and I Love Perhaps You Ask Why)

Catullus is in conflict.

Hate hate hate hate hate hate hate hate hate.
Hate hate hate hate hate hate hate love hate.
Love love love love love love love love love.
Love hate love love love love love love love.
Why why why why why why why why why why.
Why why why why why I why why why why why.
I I I I I I I I I I I I I I I I I I I I I I I I I I I I I I I I I.
I I I I I I I I I I I I I I why I I I I I I I I I I I I I I I I.

Quintia Formosast Multis (Quintia Is Beautiful to Many)

Catullus compares a certain Quintia to his own love.

There was a whiteness in you.
That kitten washed in another world look.
Good strong handshake for a girl but.
But.

Si Quicquam Mutis Gratum Acceptumve Sepulcris
(If Anything to the Silent Grave)

Catullus consoles Calvus on the death of his wife.

As tree shapes from mist
Her young death
Loose
In you.

Non Quicquam Referre Putavi (I Thought It No Matter)

Catullus is in a disparaging mood.

I've been looking up words for "anus" to describe Aemilianus'
Mouth.
Arse.
Ass.
Breech.
Bum.
Butt.
Butt-hole.
Buttock.
Caudal appendage.
Croup.
Crupper.
Dorsal root.
Fundament.
Hindgut.
Posterior opening of the alimentary canal.
Rectal redbud.
Rump.
Umiak.
Withers.
Umiak?
Smell it.

Multas per Gentes et Multa per Aequora Vectus
                (Through Peoples Through Oceans Have I Come)

Catullus buries his brother.

Multitudes brushed past me oceans I don't know.

Brother wine milk honey flowers.

Flowers milk honey brother wine.

How long does it take the sound to die away?

I a brother.

Cut out carefully the words for wine milk honey flowers.

Drop them into a bag.

Mix carefully.

Pour onto your dirty skeleton.

What sound?

Iucundum Mea Vita Mihi Proponis Amorem
                (You Promise Me My Love That This Our Love)

The poet prays for length of love.

In one of her ribald moments she gave me a holy medal.

"Never has it been heard that a prisoner of war wearing

this badge of salvation has been executed."

O adorable Face.

Pray for my enemy.

....

45

INTERVIEW WITH HARA TAMIKI (1950)

I: Death.

HT: Death made me grow up.

I: Love.

HT: Love made me endure.

I: Madness.

HT: Madness made me suffer.

I: Passion.

HT: Passion bewildered me.

I: Balance.

HT: Balance is my goddess.

I: Dreams.

HT: Dreams are everything now.

I: Gods.

HT: Gods cause me to be silent.

I: Bureaucrats.

HT: Bureaucrats make me melancholy.

I: Tears.

HT: Tears are my sisters.

I: Laughter.

HT: I wish I had a splendid laugh.

I: War.

HT: Ah war.

I: Humankind.

HT: Humankind is glass.

I: Why not take the shorter way home.

HT: There was no shorter way home.

....

FATHER'S OLD BLUE CARDIGAN

Now it hangs on the back of the kitchen chair
where I always sit, as it did
on the back of the kitchen chair where he always sat.

I put it on whenever I come in,
as he did, stamping
the snow from his boots.

I put it on and sit in the dark.
He would not have done this.
Coldness comes paring down from the moonbone in the sky.

His laws were a secret.
But I remember the moment at which I knew
he was going mad inside his laws.

He was standing at the turn of the driveway when I arrived.
He had on the blue cardigan with the buttons done up all the way to the top.
Not only because it was a hot July afternoon

but the look on his face—
as a small child who has been dressed by some aunt early in the morning
for a long trip

on cold trains and windy platforms
will sit very straight at the edge of his seat
while the shadows like long fingers

over the haystacks that sweep past
keep shocking him
because he is riding backwards.

....

"WHY DID I AWAKE (Flatman 3rd draft)

lonely among the sleepers." Up from the pavements of foreign cities—
thin shaft of autumn—who was it? Wandering street to street in gray-
ness, sound of feet on pavement, middle hours, thought of where to go
in. Why did I. Thought of everything as a middle, where to find an edge,
to find a height. Thought of this fog, why. Somewhere our groves lament
us, whom most they had loved, and the silver swimmer strokes silently
by, how far from shore is hard to say.

HOPPER: *CONFESSIONS*

> I hope it does not tell an obvious anecdote
> for none is intended.
>
> (Edward Hopper)

Nighthawks

I wanted to run away with you tonight
but you are a difficult woman
the rules of you—

Past and future circle round us
            now we know more now less
                        in the institute of shadows.

                        On a street black as widows
            with nothing to confess
our distances found us

the rules of you—
so difficult a woman
I wanted to run away with you tonight.

Yet I say boldly that I know that if nothing passed away, time past were not.
And if nothing were coming, time future were not.
And if nothing were, time present were not.

(Augustine, Confessions XI)

Automat

Night work
    neon milk
    powdered
    silk
Girl de luxe

Girl work
    plate glass love
    lone
    glove
Night de luxe

Girl work
    smell of black
    down
    the back
Night de luxe

Night work
    clamo
    ad te
    Domine
Girl de luxe

Let us see then, thou human soul, whether present time can be long:
for to thee is it given to see and to measure length of time.

                              (Augustine, *Confessions XI*)

....

Room in Brooklyn

This
slow
day
moves
Along the room
I
hear
its
axles
go
A gradual dazzle
upon
the
ceiling
Gives me that
racy
bluishyellow
feeling
As hours
blow
the
wide
way
Down my afternoon.

Let us not say time past was long, for we shall not find it.
It is no more. But let us say
time present was long,
because when it was present it was long.

(Augustine, Confessions XI)

The Barber Shop

It takes practice to shave the skin off the light.
Polarity
      means
          plus or
              minus
         total
night.
Penguins topple like astonished dice.
But
   New York
         barbers are good
      on
ice.
Morning swings in a moonsplashed hole.
Time
     zones
         jam together
               at
         the
pole.
His scissors blaze on open black water.
She
   likes
      the
         quiet she
              may
       be
      his
daughter.

Whatsoever of it has flown away is past.
Whatsoever remains is future.

         (Augustine, *Confessions XI*)

....

Western Motel

Pink bedspreads you say
are not pleasing to you
yet you sit very straight
till the pictures are through.

Two suitcases watch you like dogs.

You wear your hair parted
low on the right.
Mountains outside
look like beds without night.

Two suitcases watch you like dogs.

Glass is for getaway.
Hot is out there.
You seem to know
the road ends here.

Two suitcases watch you like dogs.

Future things then are not yet: and if they be not yet,
they are not. And if they are not,
they cannot be seen.
Yet foretold they may be
from things present which are already and are seen.

                          (Augustine, *Confessions XI*)

....

Office at Night

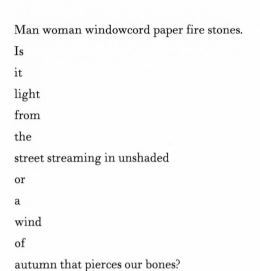

Man woman windowcord paper fire stones.
Is
it
light
from
the
street streaming in unshaded
or
a
wind
of
autumn that pierces our bones?

Yes that one hour passeth away in flying particles.
                    (Augustine, *Confessions XI*)

Summer Interior

Summer smeared the day, you slid
landing in a strange country.

So the contemplative soul—so those "dawn horses"
half-awake in the original green algae

spoke to themselves low, near
and tenderly.

I behold the daybreak, I foreshow
that the sun is about to rise.

      (Augustine, *Confessions XI*)

....

Eleven a.m.

White bones
hapless mortal
dear light of day.

Your sins do you confess them?

Covering
uncovering
where it lay.

No I keep them.

Your smile
as simple
as cloth or clay.

For rags.

From that therefore which is not yet,
through that which hath no space,
into that which now is not.

       (Augustine, *Confessions XI*)

....

Evening Wind

What dog or horse will wish to be remembered
after passing away from this world
where it moved
as a frailty.
You on the other hand creature whitely Septembered
can you pause in the thought
that links origin
and tendency?

Shut it not up I beseech thee, do not shut up these
usual yet hidden things
from my desire.

(Augustine, *Confessions XI*)

The Glove of Time by Edward Hopper

True I am but a shadow of a passenger on this planet
but my soul likes to dress in formal attire
despite the stains.
She walks through the door.
She takes off her glove.
Does she turn her head.
Does she cross her leg.
That is a question.
Who is speaking.
Also a question.
All I can say is
I see no evidence of another glove.
The words are not a sentence, don't work on that.
Work on this.
It is not empty time, it is the moment
when the curtains come blowing into the room.
When the lamp is prepared.
When light hits the wall just there.
And the glove?
Now it rose up—the life she could have lived (*par les soirs bleus d'été*).
It so happens
paint is motionless.
But if you put your ear to the canvas you will hear
the sounds of a terribly good wheel on its way.
Somewhere someone is travelling toward you,
travelling day and night.
Bare birches flow past.

· · · · · · · · · · · · · · · · ·

The red road drops away.
Here, you hold this:
evidence.
It so happens
a good evening glove
is 22 centimeters from hem to fingertip.
This was a glove "shot in the back"
(as Godard said of his *King Lear*).
Listening to his daughters Lear
hoped to see their entire bodies
stretched out across their voices
like white kid.
For in what does time differ from eternity except we measure it?

TV MEN

> TV makes things disappear. Oddly the word comes
> from Latin *videre* "to see."
>
> (Longinus, *de Sublimitate*, 5.3)

TV Men: Sappho

avec ma main brûlée j'écris sur la nature du feu

I.

No one knows what the laws are. That there are laws
we know, by the daily burnings if nothing else.
On the second

day of shooting in the Place de la Concorde
I notice the leaves in the Jardin have changed
overnight,

but mention this to no one
for fear of continuity problems.
I had already invalidated 16 (otherwise good)

takes this morning by changing an earring.
You cannot erase.
Is this a law?

No, a talent. To step obliquely
where stones are sharp.
Vice is also sharp.

There are laws against vice.
But the shock stays with you.

....

II.

la vie est brève

un peu d'amour

un peu de rêve

ainsi bonjour

The Talent has a talent
for the obvious.
See this rope?

Tie one end to me
and the other to Death:
overlit on all fours I shall

circle Him
at a consistent focal length.
Not too close not too far—

("Home," whispers the cameraman)
as the gravestones in the background
spill slowly

out of the frame.
Earth will be warmer than we thought,
after all this circling.

SEMAINE D'ARTAUD

They gave me a week to "get" Artaud and come up with a script.
Those nights were like saints.

SEE NEXT PAGE FOR DIAGRAM.

Lundi:	Folie
Mardi:	Chair
Mercredi:	Vissage
Jeudi:	Mexique
Vendredi:	De[Vol]rrida
Samedi:	Sang
Dimanche:	Éternel

Artaud is mad. He stays close to the madness. Watching it
breathe or not breathe,
he deduces laws of rhythm, which he divulges to his actors.
They are to achieve a mastery
of passions mathematically—be Artaud only sane. Observe the minutest
push and pull within themselves of muscles grazed by emotion.
Learn to render these
as breath.
Discover all that is "feminine," all that reaches forward
in supplication within us—
the way a diver digs his heels into the ocean floor in order to rise
to the surface: there is
a sudden vacuum where before there was
tension.

For Artaud the real drawback of being mad is not that consciousness
is crushed and torn but that he cannot say so,
fascinating as this would be, *while it is happening.*
But only
later when somewhat "recovered" and so much less convincingly.

The mad state is, as he emphasizes over and over again, *empty.*
Teeming with emptiness. Knotted on emptiness. Immodest in its
emptiness. You can pull emptiness out of it by the handful.
"I am not here. I am not here and never will be."
You can pull it out endlessly.

le théâtre est le seul endroit au monde où un geste fait ne se recommence
deux fois

....

A primary characteristic of pain is its demand for an explanation.

> Knife wounds.
>
> Assault with an iron bar.
>
> Shock treatments.
>
> Stigmata.
>
> Scraping.

He expresses satisfaction.

A large part of his correspondence is addressed to doctors and their wives.

J'ai mal implies   *on m'a fait mal.*

His favorite text from Van Gogh's letters to Theo describes drawing as a passage

> through an iron wall
>
> by force of will.
>
> For "will" Artaud reads *clou.*

une heure pour le caillot

He makes profound use of his face.

It is something of fire on which his soul wrote.

Portraits show an icy dandy.

Modelled by drugs and deprivation it took on an allure.

Screams are heard in the most up-to-date hospitals.

Taps his little leather heels together in the snow.

(Look over there, look down. Look at me. Not too sad. That's good.

Bit of a smile? There it is. That's what I like. Now very pensive.

Eyes lower. Now look up. More. Yes. Yes.)

Psychiatry was invented as a defense against visionaries.

Poetry (he lifts the plastic to show me)

comes from a black lump within the body, sweats itself out.

Body is pure.

Everything loathsome is the mind,

which God screws into body with a lascivious thrust.

Here is a sketch of himself as bones

dated December 1948 (he died in March).

And a bit of lung for flashing light up

onto the face from underneath.

I beg you.

ne me represente en aucune façon

In Mexico it is useful to have the obsession of counting.

For he gets lost in the membrane

which shone like pulverized sun

and only by "adding up shadows" can he find his way back

to strange centers—

from the dirty yellow table at which he sits

to what it was on the forest floor,

servant full of pity *Brueghel red,*

blood of all that matter has endured

before Artaud.

Like many a white man here he wants to believe in

God's birth.

Stare at it for hours.

car je fus Inca mais pas roi

The unique, as Derrida puts it, eludes discourse. Artaud's adventure resists clinical or critical exegesis, it is a protest against exemplification itself. Artaud habitually destroys the history of himself as an example, history of a difference between his body and his mind, history that doctors and critics are combing and scouring after to comment on it. He wants both to speak and to forbid his speech being spirited away (*soufflée:* Derrida) and placed in an order of truth for commentary. "Artaud knew that all speech fallen from the body, offering itself to understanding or reception, offering itself as spectacle, is stolen speech." To speak in such a way that the theft blocks itself. His theater of cruelty is where he stages public attempts at this. But the prior stage is mind. "Something is destroying my thinking, something furtive which takes away from me the words which I found." To have thoughts *which even he himself will not want to steal* and repeat as speech. He must become so boring or abhorrent to himself that his language does not eavesdrop on its own calls.

kilzi

trakilzi

faildor

barabama

baraba

mince
o dedi

o dada orzoura

o dou zoura

o dada skizi

What holes, and made of what?

To the scandal of language he does not consent.

False etymology makes him bold.

He says *unglue words from the sky:*

Car après, dit poématique, après viendra le temps du sang.
Puisqu'ema, en grec, veut dire sang, et que po-ema
doit vouloir dire
après
le sang
le sang après.
Faisons d'abord poème, avec sang.

For after, said poetically, after will come the time of blood.

Since *ema* in Greek means "blood," and *po-ema*

ought to mean

"after

the blood"

"the blood after."

Let us make first *poem*, with blood.

Violence is total here. He deliberately misspells

the ancient Greek word for "poem" (*poiema*)

as "poema."

Then misdivides it

into *po* and *ema* (2 nonexistent syllables in Greek),

wrongly identifying *ema* with the Greek word for "blood" (*haima*)

in order to etymologize *poema* as "after the blood after"

(but in what language does *po* mean "after"?)

Poetically indeed.

mais j'en ai assez ce sera pour un prochain livre

. . . .

He died at dawn on 4th March.

With spring snow on the ground.

Alone in his pavilion. Seated at the foot of his bed.

Holding his shoe.

His body did not burst into unforgettable fragments at his death, no.

That summer was throughout Europe remarkable for its tempests.

Here I am! What lightning! was what people said

as they strolled along.

et en effet c'est trop peu pour moi

....

TV Men: Artaud

Artaud is mad.

He stayed close to the madness. Watching it breathe or not breathe.

There is a close-up of me driven to despair.

His face is mad.

It was something of fire on which his soul wrote. All this mental glass.

Me beating my head against a wall.

His body is mad.

Some days he felt uterine. Mind screwed into him by a thrust of sky.

I run among the ruins.

His mind is mad.

There was (he decided) no mind. The body (hell) just as you see it.

Go throw myself from the tower, gesticulating, falling.

His hospital is mad.

He noted in electric shock a splash state. What holes, and made of what?

Falling to the beach.

His Mexico is mad.

There was not a shadow he did not count. No opium, no heads on the days.

You see my body crumpled on the sand.

His God is mad.

He felt God pulling him out through his own cunt. Claque. Claque-dents.

It moves convulsively a few times.

....

73

His double is mad.

The drawback of being mad was that he could not both be so and say so.

Beautiful jerks.

His word is mad.

He had to become an enigma to himself. To prevent his own theft of him.

You see my battered face.

His excrement is mad.

He envied bones their purity. Hated to die *rectified* (as he said) by pain.

Then I fall back.

His spring snow is mad.

They found him at dawn. Seated at the foot of his bed. Holding his shoe.

And shy away.

TV Men: Tolstoy

I. CHAMBRE

A curiously tender man and yet
even after their marriage he
called his desire to kiss her
"the appearance of Satan."

Her in right profile against the light, all the music in the room streams
toward the blue frosty window.

Desire, the trees are rags. Desire, streaks of it
scalding the fog. This is not what I meant (Lev thinks wildly)—
words from a bad play, embraces that knock the lamp,
you are so young! And this fog.

His bedroom on a March morning as cool as pearls, close-up on rustling,
coats or shawls.

Lev had no death wish.

He was on a grand voyage through the colors of men and women, crime, madness and courage.

Never mind! many a drunk coachman advised him.

So what!

That's how it is! Life! Well all right!

No need for better!

You'll live you'll see!

Lev continues to pour out sacks onto the zinc table, to run his fingers through grain after grain, handful after handful. No night ever has enough.

The horse named Délire, that was not enough.

III. CORPS

In sex (he told her) the mind evaporates and suddenly
the body is there,
just the body with its reaches.
He was more or less repulsive to himself,
the little satin parts especially.

Her alone at a midnight table in the zala, *leaning over the manuscript with
her shortsighted eyes, shadow of her bent arm huge on the wall.*

Take notes with your eyes, he advises. War is clear and intricate.
Lev watched a shell fall
near a boy and girl
playing horse in the street.

Boy and girl hold their arms about one another and fall down together.

Gambling wildly that night at the officers' club, Lev loses
his ancestral home
whose central section,
with balconies and staircases,
has to be rebuilt on the property of its new owner
a few towns away.
Back from the war, Lev announces Emancipation to his serfs
who craftily
reject the plan.
The two remaining sections of his house,
now connected by empty space and a string of bushes,
have a raw feel.

Riding back at evening to his very quiet house he smells spring in the lime trees, he is alone.

V. FAIM

When famine struck Lev moved like a lion
from village to village, passing out bread,
sleeping in a bare hut. Over two years he
set up 248 soup kitchens. Asked
this vast country,
Are we our brother's keeper?

(The government considered confining him to a fortress
which he would have loved.)

Now he was ploughing and the world was watching.
Tolstoy Ploughing (by Repin) shows him
hunched over the brown earth, seeing no flesh.

His calves as sleek as otters.

When he got round to rebuilding the middle of his house
Lev made a school.
The state schools outraged him.
In place of rote memory and flogging Lev declared
the free child.

DO AS YOU LIKE reads a sign over the door.

Sometimes all forty small scholars spent the night
in his study.
No books, he just talked. A lot about war.
"Hardly anyone could help shuddering
at his descriptions," a student recalls.
At noon they went out to throw snowballs.
"Who can knock me down?" cried Lev springing over the snow.
Later he referred to this time as "the clear glade."
In some ways he was never so happy.
Sitting on the porch with his students in the evening
Lev told of his desire
to divide up his land
and live like a peasant.
"Like you," he said.

Small scholars sit silent, regarding the lively colors of his night.

VII. LIBERTÉ

Lev could lift 180 lbs. with one hand.
In a mowing mood he would go out to the fields
and borrow a scythe from whoever looked most tired.
Yet a peasant can mow for 6 days on end
eating rye bread and sleeping
on cold ground (he mused).
"They know how to die,"
he often said as if it were a freedom.
Freedom for landowners came from another direction.
The railroad: 16,700 versts of track by 1876.
Destroys the woods, pulls people from labor,
and raises the price of grain! these were Lev's
objections. Yet
from a sad local event
came the exposed skull bone
of Anna Karenina.

Night plasters leaves against the station door.

VIII. NUIT DIVINE

Live a true life?
His *Diary for Myself Alone* records misgivings.
"After an enormous dinner with champagne
(the Tanyas all dressed in white) our cart
pushed its way toward the forest for a picnic,
through crowds of peasants coming back
exhausted from work."
Alone at night Lev could feel the divine fire pouring out his eyes.
But the day with its doors, accusations, tomatoes,
with its rosemilk breasts of girls,
rain, cold, mad people and heartburn—
wore him to the nub.
"Whist in the evening and a feeling of shame."

*Him writing then laying down his pen, hot smell of onions pervading the
room.*

At the end of the first notebook of *Diary for Myself Alone*
a sheet of paper is pasted in. Her hand:
"I copy this sad diary of my husband.
So much here is—may God forgive me—
unjust cruel untruthful dragged up invented.
Let good people read how he was when he courted me.
'I am in love as never before . . . I shall shoot myself' etc.
Then he was My Lev."

*Back of her head, in the lamplight the old scarred wooden table looks red
as a cockscomb.*

. . . .

IX. FAMILLE

When the dark people began appearing
he spoke to everyone. Door ajar.
Then it eased his heart to go down to the river
and chop wood with the peasants.
How the family depressed him.
"With their joys—music furniture shopping!"
On bad days he threw a few things
into a knapsack and left for America.

Looking for mushrooms, he mumbles coming back through the zala *a few hours later.*

X. VOUS AUTRE

With the diaries he forced into her
a jealousy that licked her insides
for 47 years.
They both wrote every night.
"Immortal wheat for the New Life!" begins his entry for June 2, 1837.
And next door,
with her little red reading glasses perched on her nose,
"If I could kill him then make another man exactly like him,
I would do it joyfully!"

Her leaving a doorway, light leaving a doorway.

XI. MORT

There is a dog howling in Russia's soul.
"Imagine him in his coffin, he lies like a smooth stone
at the bottom of a stream,"
said Gorky when Lev died.
Spring snow fell shyly from a light red sky.
Four thousand peasants turned up carrying a banner
YOUR GOODNESS WILL NOT DIE OUT AMONG US DEAR LEV.
An old man whom no one knew spoke briefly.
The coffin was lowered.
Policemen knelt.
There are lamps we cannot light here
(we can light them later).
What have we prayed for if not for this?
Slowly silently the crowd moved away.

Voronka River goes on caressing its banks.

XII. FIN

"Indeed the pit bears iron."
After his death she dreams of roses and bones.
To have put roses under his feet! her grief
was beyond telling—to put something
there where he would fall, or a bit
of arnica for his bruises—
God's meal is a buried meal.

Fields alone, fields standing, all night they are there. Men of old have sung.

TV Men: Lazarus

DIRECTOR OF PHOTOGRAPHY: VOICEOVER

Yes I admit a degree of unease about my
motives in making
this documentary.
Mere prurience of a kind that is all too common nowadays
in public catastrophes. I was listening

to a peace negotiator for the Balkans talk
about his vocation
on the radio the other day.
"We drove down through this wasteland and I didn't know
much about the area but I was

fascinated by the horrors of it. I had never
seen a thing like this.
I videotaped it.
Then sent a 13-page memo to the UN with my suggestions."
This person was a member

of the International Rescue Committee,
not a man of TV.
But you can see
how the pull is irresistible. The pull to handle horrors
and to have a theory of them.

But now I see my assistant producer waving her arms

at me to get

on with the script.

The name Lazarus is an abbreviated form of Hebrew *'El'azar*,

meaning "God has helped."

I have long been interested in those whom God has helped.

It seems often to be the case,

e.g. with saints or martyrs,

that God helps them to far more suffering than they would have

without God's help. But then you get

someone like Lazarus, a man of no

particular importance,

on whom God bestows

the ultimate benevolence, without explanation, then abandons

him again to his nonentity.

We are left wondering, *Why Lazarus?*

My theory is

God wants us to wonder this.

After all, if there were some quality that Lazarus possessed,

some criterion of excellence

by which he was chosen to be called

back

from death,

then we would all start competing to achieve this.

But if

....

God's gift is simply random, well
for one thing
it makes a
more interesting TV show. God's choice can be seen emerging
from the dark side of reason

like a new planet. No use being historical
about this planet,
it is just an imitation.
As Lazarus is an imitation of Christ. As TV is an imitation of
Lazarus. As you and I are an imitation of

TV. Already you notice that
although I am merely
a director of photography,
I have grasped certain fundamental notions first advanced by Plato,
e.g. that our reality is just a TV set

inside a TV set inside a TV set, with nobody watching
but Sokrates,
who changed
the channel in 399 B.C. But my bond with Lazarus goes deeper, indeed
nausea overtakes me when faced with

the prospect of something simply beginning all over again.
Each time I have to
raise my slate and say
"Take 12!" or "Take 13!" and then "Take 14!"
I cannot restrain a shudder.

....

Repetition is horrible. Poor Lazarus cannot have known
he was an
imitation Christ,
but who can doubt he realized, soon after being ripped out of his
warm little bed in the ground,

his own epoch of repetition just beginning.
Lazarus Take 2!
Poor drop.
As a bit of salt falls back down the funnel. Or maybe my pity
is misplaced. Some people think Lazarus lucky,

like Samuel Beckett who calls him "Happy Larry" or Rilke
who speaks of
that moment in a game
when "the pure too-little flips over into the empty too-much."
Well I am now explaining why my documentary

focuses entirely on this moment, the flip-over moment.
Before and after
don't interest me.
You won't be seeing any clips from home videos of Lazarus
in short pants racing his sisters up a hill.

No footage of Mary and Martha side by side on the sofa
discussing how they manage
at home
with a dead one sitting down to dinner. No panel of experts
debating who was really the victim here.

....

Our sequence begins and ends with that moment of complete
innocence
and sport—
when Lazarus licks the first drop of afterlife off the nipple
of his own old death.

I put tiny microphones all over the ground
to pick up
the magic
of the vermin in his ten fingers and I stand back to wait
for the miracle.

How does a body do in the ground?

Clouds look like matted white fur.
Which are the animals? He has forgotten the difference
between near and far.
Round pink ones come at him.
From the pinks shoot fluids
some dark (from eyes) some loud (from mouth).

His bones are moving like a mist in him

all blown to the surface then sideways.
I do not want to see,
he thinks in pain
as a darkish clump
cuts across his field of vision,
and some
strange

silver milk
is filling the space,
gets caught in the mist,
twists all his bones to the outside where they ignite in air.
The burning
of his bones

lets Lazarus know where each bone is.

....

And so
shifted forward into solidity—
although he pulls against it and groans to turn away—
Lazarus locks on
with a whistling sound behind him
as panels slide shut

and his soul congeals on his back in chrysolite drops

which almost at once evaporate.
Lazarus
(someone is calling his name)—his name!
And at the name (which he knew)
not just a roar of darkness
the whole skeletal freight

of him
took pressure,
crushing him backward into the rut where he lay
like a damp
petal
under a pile of furniture.

And the second fact of his humanity began.

For the furniture shrank upon him as a bonework of
not just volume but
secret volume—
where fingers go probing
into drawers

....

and under
pried-up boxlids,

go rifling mute garments of white

and memories are streaming from his mind to his heart—
of someone standing at the door.
Of white breath in frozen air.
Mary. Martha.
Linen of the same silence.
Lazarus! (again the voice)
and why not

climb the voice

where it goes spiralling upward
lacing him on a glow point
into the nocturnal motions of the world so that he is
standing now
propped on a cage of hot pushes of other people's air
and he feels more than hears
her voice (again)

like a salt rubbed whole into raw surface—

Lazarus!
A froth of fire is upon his mind.
It crawls to the back of his tongue,
struggles a bit,
cracking the shell

....

and pushes out a bluish cry that passes at once to the soul.
Martha!

he cries, making a little scalded place

on the billows of tomb that lap our faces as we watch.
We know the difference now
(life or death).
For an instant it parts our hearts.
Someone take the linen napkin off his face,
says the director quietly.

GIOTTO SHOT LIST

1—

At the window someone is waving his hand like a windblown branch.
It is Giotto.
His hard fresh eyes see the weights of things.
His Lazarus blows
against
the north wall of the Scrovegni Chapel.
Stuck like
a seed.
Two laborers
stagger as they set the stone slab of the tomb
down.

2—

By drawing a listener aside out of earshot

Giotto creates

foreground and background.

Lazarus there you come stained with ordinary death,

a white grub tottering.

So young, such a terrible actor.

Life pulls softly inside your bindings.

The pod glows

—dear stench.

Hoods turn away.

Not a whisper in the noonblue as

Giotto slips

you

sideways into time.

Wrist-thick on the plain a sapling bends.

3—

Now you must get rid of the ideas *crude* and *violent,* think:
Some gigantic opal.
Tints resembling iridescence have the strange quality of
imprisoned life.
How dare Giotto arrange this pure staring color?
I paint the original shell.
It is Giotto who first let sky into paintings.
Away with this gold!
Compare the decaying fire of Byzantium with Giotto's
lime plaster day.
Fresco is fast and a little cold. It gives an impression
of fact,
due to perfect carbonation of wet pigment with God's
will.

4—

Bandaged head to foot in pieces of diagonal cloth,
Lazarus flickers
between two heavily veiled people like a bit of kindling
or a stalk
of something white and dry stuck in the ground.
His eyes
have the power of the other world. Barely open,
narrow shock slits
whose gaze is directed—simply, nowhere.
It drifts
in a chill space left by other gazes intersecting on
his not there.
Meanwhile God on the other side of the painting is
sending
the whole heat of His love of Man across the wall
in a glance,
toward Lazarus' cheekbones still radiant with a
"studio light"
that twangs faintly on the day. Shadow if you
pay attention
to it too long will climb into your eyes and whiten
real objects.

TV Men: Antigone (Scripts 1 and 2)

Antigone likes walking behind Oedipus
to brake the wind.
As he is blind he often does not agree to this.
March sky cold as a hare's paw.
Antigone and Oedipus eat lunch on the lip of a crater.
Trunks of hundred-year-old trees forced
down
by wind
crawl on the gravel. One green centimeter of twig
still vertical—
catches her eye. She leads his hand to it.
Lightly
he made sure
what it was.
Lightly left it there.

[Antigone felt a sting against her cheek. She motions the soundman out of the way and taking the microphone begins to speak.]

There is nowhere to keep anything, the way we live.
This I find hard. Other things I like—a burnish
along the butt end of days
that people inside houses never see.
Projects, yes I have projects.
I want to make a lot of money. *Just kidding. Next*
question. No I do not lament.
God's will is not some sort of physics, is it.

Today we are light, tomorrow shadow, says the song.
Ironic? Not really. My father is the ironic one.
I have my own ideas about it.
At our backs is a big anarchy.
If you are strong you can twist a bit off
and pound on it—your freedom!

Now Oedipus has risen, Antigone rises. He begins to move off,
into the wind,
immersed in precious memory.
Thinking *Too much memory* Antigone comes after.
Both of them are gold all along the sunset side.
Last bell, he knew.
Among all fleshbags you will not find
one who if God
baits
does not bite.

[For sound-bite purposes we had to cut Antigone's script from 42 seconds to 7:
substantial changes of wording were involved but we felt we got her "take"
right.]

Other things I like: a lot of money!
The way we live, light and shadow are ironic.
Projects? yes: physics. Anarchy. My father.
Here, twist a bit off.
Freedom is next.

TV Men: Akhmatova (Treatment for a Script)

AKHMATOVA'S MARRIAGE (1910) HAS LITTLE EFFECT ON HER

Do you love him? I don't know. I believe he is my fate.
        Inside the church ikons glowed vastly.
Out on the steps the fog hustled people away, in groups or alone.
        At last only she was left. She had tossed her wing
over one arm. Poetry has no such use,
        and starkly paced inside her.

NOT A WIFE BUT A WITCH, WRITES HUSBAND GUMILYOV (1912)

Afternoon grays over shot gold—the Schönberg color—
        and noiseless winterblasted crows halt on branches that
                resent them halting. Below sat Akhmatova with her
        symbols as if on soft pillows. Little sinner
of a sunbeam wandered onto her.

LITTLE LEV GOES TO LIVE WITH GRANDMOTHER IN THE COUNTRY

Earliest spring light the color of beaten egg white
      on a scalded hull of sky, now blue now stuffed
           with bleachy cloud chasm after chasm falling
               by. Akhmatova's knees were warm in the sun
           but her back felt cold as an old burying ground.
      Anechka you are young and pretty what do you need a baby for?
they said, wrapping the nestling in stages of eternity.

....

HOW CLOSE WAS AKHMATOVA WITH HER FATHER IS HARD TO SAY

She sometimes visited him.

Was there when he died.

In a transparent city they drank mortal air side by side.

That was the summer of 1914.

Streaks darkened the walls.

From bed he kept asking her to telephone the navy and ask

if Viktor might come home soon (his son).

LULLS AND BETRAYALS

Eerie cranes and leafless trees evoke the blasted marriage.

What have you done with me? he asks.

I have repeated you.

REMEMBERING THE DAY THE WINTER PALACE WAS TAKEN (1917)

Gods of the revolution came one October night from Finland.

She saw blood flow on snow and stones.

But by November

they had licked the Tsars off Russia clean as a cow's tongue.

When torpedo boats came up the river to support them

Akhmatova saw the Liteyny Bridge—never before in

daylight—

raised: trucks trams people everything suddenly hanging over

the break. Blossoms

stare at the camera.

DIVORCE IN GENERAL IS A VERY DIFFICULT THING

March threw its knives against the door.

Gumilyov bit her hands. Why have you made this up?

He moved to Ivanovsky Street, he moved

into a net. All his subsequent failures

can be traced here. Including marriage

to another woman named Anna.

SECOND HUSBAND, A SCHOLAR

Rations were hard to get, she stood in line for apples and matches.

While in their cold apartment he went on translating

Babylonian texts.

Petersburg was no longer the capital (Moscow was).

Behind

the signboards—damp darkness.

Hands broke off statues.

People pillaged even the cemeteries.

The Commission for the Improvement of Artists' Lives

was serving cheap soup and pellets of bread

to evening writers in boots and shawls

and Laplander earflaps.

Over soup more than one person said to her, You stun me.

The dog has become old, whispered Akhmatova then.

Back at home the scholar had got the skin off

several unknown words.

His incisions made a dull blue sound like silk.

TELEPHONE LANGUAGE (1925)

You know quiver is held up at the printer's
        meant Gumilyov had been arrested.
From Cheka headquarters he was taken to Gorokhovaya
        (the other prison) and from there to a grove on the Iriniskaya Road.
A small curved pine, next to it another with torn roots.
        This was the wall meant
sixty people were shot there.
        Two pits. The earth sank down.

CAMPAIGN AGAINST AKHMATOVA BEGINS (1922)

She ran from lamppost to lamppost, the wind slammed.
Trotsky reviewed her in *Pravda: One reads with dismay* . . .
and an unofficial Communist Party resolution banned her poetry (1925).
She didn't notice, didn't know what a Communist Party was in those days.
Fog choked the city.
Russia's great poets were all about 35 years old.
Scraggly trees wandered by the canal in dim sun.

MANDELSTAM

Akhmatova was translating *Macbeth* in the early '30s
> (a time she called "the vegetarian years" to distinguish
>> its charm from "the meat-eating years" still ahead).

For a poem in which he likened Stalin's fingers to worms
> Osip Mandelstam was arrested in May 1934. All night
>> the police searched his papers and threw them

out on the floor
> to the sound of a ukelele
>> from the next apartment.

Akhmatova never finished *Macbeth* although
> she liked to quote the hero saying people
>> in my homeland die faster than

the flowers on their hats.

AKHMATOVA COMES TO THE WALL

Real Terror began in December 1934.

Song bees by the thousand vanishing as the Kremlin clock struck twelve.
> Akhmatova—weep now,

"but the moisture boiled off before it reached my eyes."

Akhmatova's son Lev was arrested in 1933 (released), 1935 (released),
> 1938 (not released).

She came to the wall to stand in line.

Inner prison of the NKVD on Shpalernaya Street.
> Then Kresty Prison across the Neva.

Once a month a window opened in the wall.

Akhmatova—for Gumilyov, she said
> shoving her parcel through the grate.

THREE HUNDREDTH IN LINE WITH A PARCEL

"It smells of burning."
> The mother remains alone.
>> The wall is subtly different from hour to hour. Season to
>> season.
>>> Whitish.
>>>> Scalded.
>>> Sprayed with dawn.
>> Beasts passing.
> Laid her ear to the wall, heard people working one another on the
anvil, did not listen again.

SHE HAS TO MEMORIZE THEN BURN ALL POEMS PERTAINING TO THE WALL

Night rested its paws on the top of the wall.
"The purpose of terrorism is terror" (Lenin).

SIEGE

In March 1940 dark disconnected lines of verse
> began to appear on the margins of her manuscripts.
>> Slowly they wandered out with their wounds, she
let them rest there. Saw they were a woman
> setting off on "the way of all the earth."
>> Under the iron roof at night she lay listening
to their wooden legs go tapping up the sidewalk,
> woman heading east along the canal toward
> the sour-milk smell of Asia.
>> Last things she saw as she left Leningrad were
today the wall with a long soaked mark on it.

....

RETURN TO LENINGRAD WHERE EVEN THE SHADES HAVE DIED
OF HUNGER (1944)

Borders trembled all around her.
She saw friends by now gone mad with wolvish grins.
"This is some terrible mistake."
Poking past smashed glass of her apartment
      she sat
on a rusty bedspring
which sank to the ground.
A tart smell of sacred oak came to her
whispering Pushkin's most daring line,
      Into the darkness of someone else's garden. . . .

AKHMATOVA REMEMBERS HER VISIT TO THE MEYERHOLDS (1935)

The family was struck by grief, they didn't know
      how Vsevolod was faring.
Asked her to find out. She went to the wall
      and knocked on the window. Like to know
what happened with Meyerhold. She could see
      a man in stained uniform leafing through a huge register.
Moving his lips. Meyerhold, Meyerhold, let me see.
      That's it . . . here you are. . . . Executed. His blank
eyes regarded her throat or collar. He was
      chewing something.

You're guilty! In what form would you like to confess this?

they said to Lev at the interrogation. They did not beat him much.

Sentenced him to 10 years in Karaganda region, correspondence limited.

Akhmatova burned all her papers—manuscripts, notebooks, letters—

and began the tale of two cities:

Leningrad to Moscow

every month

to hand in a parcel of food at the little window in the wall

(8 kilos maximum including the box).

Accepted, it meant he was still alive.

AKHMATOVA REPENTS (1950)

How could she save her son except by praising Stalin?

"Along the once demolished highway,

light autos now fly."

Her cycle of Socialist Realist poems was published in Moscow in

Ogonyok.

Amid the unending tundra Lev labored on.

Her head was covered that day by a large black seeing scar.

She walked like someone in the ashes of a house, stopping.

On hot days we loved to hide here. Pointing. *Like mortals.*

Not poisoned when he left (1949) from Lefortovo Prison (Moscow)
> to Karaganda region for ten years hard labor.
>> She spent those long years trying to get him free.
> But she was a writer under Decree.

One Wednesday (1956) he turned up
> unannounced at her door.
>> Lev smokes like a chimney!
> Akhmatova was jubilant at first,

waving fumes toward the window of the small kitchen where she
> lived. Lev had balanced 14 years
>> on a bloodaxe, now he
> spoke in monosyllables and didn't like her friends—"dead grapes"

who steamed up his glasses with their Lyova! Lyovushka! and their
endless
> tiny cups of tea.
>> Spirits passing on the border saw flesh and blood and blame
>> darken the kitchen like torture.

After a quarrel she had a heart attack.
> You've always been ill, said Lev and got accommodation
>> on the other side of the city.
> And those walls saturated with thoughts of him—

with dreams, insomnia, declarations,
> summonses, petitions, meetings,
>> nonmeetings, fevers,
> mortifications,

if-clauses,
> hairs
>> placed in a notebook—are still there to see.

From cunning life she always took what she needed for her craft.

Night stained her inbetween the stove and the dresser.

Now it rose up—the life

she could have lived (simple, with bees and neighbors, a backfence),

the cities that changed their names or burned,

silence (whip).

She spent the 1960s trying to reconstruct a play *Enuma Elish*
(When Above . . .)

that she had begun in Tashkent, then destroyed.

"No ashes are left." She begged her friends

to recall some fragment, the creak of the well, she, he.

Her vision was of something between Kafka and Chaplin,

white lines on black velvet, Symbolist farce.

All she got was a pile of fish heads.

Wrapped them in a newspaper of 1946 and called it

Dream within a Dream.

"Eat the food, Enkidu,

as life requires.

Drink the wine, as is the custom of

the land."

KOMAROVO IS AKHMATOVA'S FINAL HOME

Outside the little hut in the writers' colony of Komarovo were
        pine trees and lilac bushes.
She worked at a desk made out of an attic door and slept on bricks.
        "Pushkin's mattress
stood on birch logs, mine is on eight bricks."
        She loved noise and had many guests,
famous ones, old friends, mad persons, with pinecones, with lilacs,
        on motorcycles, in dazzling white.
She made trips—to Italy (for a prize) and Oxford (for a doctorate)
        with a companion (female)
and many small bottles of nitroglycerin. Home again
        she liked to build a bonfire in the yard
and sit on an old armchair, drink 2 or 3 glasses of vodka, watch it go
        far into the night—something miraculous
even from the altitude of the mid-twentieth century! particles
        thrown off by a soul as it cools.

IT SO HAPPENS (1966)

Akhmatova was surrounded on her deathbed by women
    scheming to get control of her papers.
        Akuma used to eat our bread, they said firmly.
            Lev was kept out of the room in case seeing him killed her.
        It so happens death killed her
on a March morning when the wind was snatching at the panes
full of sounds, not voices but like voices
    as she rode up, rode over.
        When your horse decides on the hill you can feel
          his hindlegs sink—
            observe this moment.

....

Began to develop script in 1957. Wrote to Akhmatova in Leningrad. Applied for TV license at that time. Application denied. How to get permission to reapply for TV license. Attend funeral of artist Osmyorkin. Snow is falling on the birch trees. Talk to Rudnev (architect renovating Moscow University). Rudnev knows Voroshilov (military marshal and onetime Stalinist). Wait 3 months. Snow is falling on the highway and on the fields. Draft a letter. Gershtein takes letter to Rudnev who telephones Voroshilov's personal assistant. Assistant agrees to give letter to Voroshilov. Next day accompany Gershtein to guardhouse at Trinity Gate (Kremlin) to hand over letter. Snow is falling in the rearview mirror. Wait half a year. Late August, letter from TV Prosecutor saying no grounds for reexamining application. Twice to TV Prosecutor's office, no result. Snow is falling on Cicero's head, and on his hands. Months pass. Persuade several academics to write letters. Snow is falling with a jittery blue glow in it. Scholar Struve drafts petition describing my TV work (leaving out name of sponsors). Snow is falling on bonfires in the back parking lot. Struve sends petition with supporting materials directly to Ringmaster, no result. Snow is falling on lambs in the moonlight. Gershtein makes appointment with TV Prosecutor to ask whether Struve's letter has been sent there from Ringmaster's office. Told to come back in a month. Returns, told yes it arrived. Returns following month. Returns following month. Month. Month. Snow is falling on the *Wingless Victory* outside the train station that people mistake for Catherine the Great. Petition under consideration. December, still no response. Snow is falling on swans asleep on the canal. Gershtein and Struve make appointment with director of Hermitage in Moscow (he knows me, *old style*). Get very strong letter. This could be it. Hopes are high. Receive news of Akhmatova's death in Komarovo.

....

. . .

I suppose I could have made the film anyhow—what can I say. Combat went out of me. Spring snow looks wrong in the late light of evening, yet it continues to fall, filling the crater, covering altars and pits, drifting up almost as high as the stain on the wall, blotting out all trace of the harvest.

TV Men: Thucydides in Conversation with Virginia Woolf
on the Set of The Peloponnesian War

T: Bell dies away in seven seconds then a light comes up and we see you walking.

VW: Can you explain the walking again.

T: Begin right with the right foot, left with the left, each time nine steps right to left and back again.

VW: Does she do this every day.

T: Yes it is routine.

VW: Without feeling.

T: Routine.

VW: When does she speak.

T: Fourth step. First sentence ends immediately before the turn.

VW [walking]: *War costs are of two kinds direct and indirect.*

T: When you walk slump together. When you speak straighten up a bit.

VW: *War costs are of two kinds direct and indirect. Direct costs embrace all expenditures made by belligerents in carrying on hostilities.*

T: Too much color. No movements with the head. Monotone, very distant.

VW: *War costs are of two kinds direct and indirect. Direct costs embrace all expenditures made by belligerents in carrying on hostilities. Indirect costs—*

....

T: It's an improvisation not a story. You're looking for words, correct yourself constantly. Voice of an epilogue.

VW: *War costs are of two kinds direct and indirect. Direct costs embrace all expenditures made by belligerents in carrying on hostilities. Indirect costs include economic loss from death—*

T: That's a terrible singsong now. Tone has to be colder. But tense.

VW: *War costs are of two kinds direct and—*

T: Perhaps we should time the lips' movements.

VW: *War costs are of two kinds direct and indirect. Direct—*no.

T: You're looking for the tone, that's fatal. Think visionary. Try again from "death."

VW: ... *death, property damage, reduced production, war relief and the like. For example, direct costs of the European War 1914–1918 are estimated at $186,333,637,097 and indirect costs at—*

T: Keep the tension.

VW [voice rising]: *$151,646,942,560 bringing the total war bill to $337,980,579,657 (calculated in U.S. dollars) for all participants!*

T: Not quite. Remember you feel cold the whole time. Your body too. North wind and night.

VW: How about a cigarette.

T: And not too sad it should under no circumstances sound tragic. Perhaps I'll leave you alone awhile.

VW [walking and whispering]: *Notwithstanding these figures the First World War was fought mainly on credit.*

T: Lip movements should be roughly the same length. In fact one is twenty-two seconds, the other twenty-four.

VW: *Hence the Second World War.*

T: Can we play with that strip of light.

TV Men: Sappho

Sappho is smearing on her makeup at 5 a.m. in the woods by the hotel.
He She Me You Thou disappears

Now resembling a Beijing concubine Sappho makes her way onto the set.
Laugh Breathe Look Speak Is disappears

The lighting men are setting up huge white paper moons here and there
on the grass.
Tongue Flesh Fire Eyes Sound disappears

Behind these, a lamp humming with a thousand broken wasps.
Cold Shaking Green Little Death disappears

Places everyone, calls the director.
Nearness When Down In I disappears

Toes to the line please, says the assistant cameraman.
But All And Must To disappears

Action!
Disappear disappears

Sappho stares into the camera and begins, *Since I am a poor man—*
Cut

IRONY IS NOT ENOUGH: ESSAY ON MY LIFE AS CATHERINE DENEUVE (2nd draft)

saison qui chante saison rapide

je commence

Beginnings are hard. Sappho put it simply. Speaking of a young girl Sappho said, *You burn me*. Deneuve usually begins with herself and a girl together in a hotel room. This is mental. Meanwhile the body persists. Sweater buttoned almost to the neck, she sits at the head of the seminar table expounding aspects of Athenian monetary reform. It was Solon who introduced into Athens a coinage which had a forced currency. Citizens had to accept issues called drachmas, didrachmas, obols, etc. although these did not contain silver of that value. Token coinages. Money that lies about itself. Seminar students are writing everything down carefully, one is asleep, Deneuve continues to talk about money and surfaces. Little blues, little whites, little hotel taffetas. This is mental. Bell rings to mark the end of class. *He has a foreskin but for fear of wearing it out he uses another man's when he copulates, is what Solon's enemies liked to say of him*, Deneuve concludes. *Fiscal metaphor.* She buttons her top button and the seminar is over.

jours

If you asked her Deneuve would say *Take these days away and pour them out on the ground in another country.*

parts

Seminar meets MonWedFri. Parts of time fall on her and snow wanders slowly through the other afternoons. Deneuve sits in her office looking at the word *irony* on a page. Half-burnt. You have to wonder. Sappho, Sokrates, is it all mental? These people seem bathed in goodness, yet here come the beautiful dangerous white rapids beating onto them. Knife of boy. Knife of girl. Knife of the little knower. Where is the ironic work that picks threads back from that surface into another design underneath, holding rapids in place? Evening fills the room. Deneuve buttons her coat and closes the office door behind her. Staircase is dim and filthy, small dirty deposits on each step. She heads for the Metro. What would Sokrates say. Name the parts. Define each name. Deneuve is turning names and parts over in her mind when she realizes she has ridden the train four stops in the wrong direction. Climbs back up from the platform, stairs are filthy here too, must be a punishment. Hip slams hard into the metal arm of the turnstile. Red sign pasted on it says NO EXIT. Sound is far away. All around her strange lamps burn brightly and human tongues press the night.

weekends

Weekends are long and white. Snow drifts against the door. Distant threads from the piano downstairs. Deneuve washes her glassware. Dries it. Hours slide. In the hotel room it is dusk, a girl turns, *I have to confess something.* This is mental. Two parallel red lines of different lengths inch forward, not touching.

téléphones

Shame is a rusty edge that Deneuve sits on as she pages through lecture notes in her Monday office. Outside a flag shreds itself in the icy wind. Telephone rings. Jagged pause. Girl's voice, which she has never heard before on the telephone, is animal. Claws lope through her and turn at the wall. *Not coming to seminar today. Thought you should know.* Girl stops. Deneuve waits. And then, *Do you care?* with a laugh—drops away—dangling, Deneuve grabs for an answer to that. Yes. No. No answer. Wrong answer. Wrong question. Trick question! Spins, they grapple, slip off, hold. *I plan to come Wednesday,* girl says. *Do that,* Deneuve answers. Dial tone. World sags and swings back against the void at the middle of MonWedFri. Fifty-three hours.

neiges

Snows all night, snows all day. Still snowing in midafternoon when Deneuve looks up from her papers to see a girl's ears bright red, eyebrows snowplastered. She leans in the doorway and holds up her glasses by one broken earpiece. Deneuve offers mending tape. Girl mends the earpiece, drops her coat on the floor, sits beside it. Takes out her Greek book and begins to translate, as if it had been prearranged. Had it? Deneuve feels a force of life coming at her too strong to think what parts this has or why it should happen. The victim of an ironic situation is typically innocent. Gradually twilight soaks the room, now it is almost too dark to read. Girl is lifting her coat, poised in the doorway, gone. *Thanks,* floats back along the hall. Looking down Deneuve sees her feet are naked. *Moi je comprends pas ça,* she whispers to them.

pipes

Deneuve tells the truth every Friday, it's a rule (Sokrates did too). Girl arrives at her office early, knocks over a chair and starts to cry. Trouble with her boyfriend in Paris. *Most important thing in my life.* Deneuve turns to stare out the window at a raw March morning. Do you know how diamonds get to us? Three hundred miles underground are heats and pressures that crush carbon into sparkling shapes, driven for months or days or hours along hotel corridors called diamond pipes until they erupt in a pile of taffeta and chocolate some moonlit afternoon, an event no human has ever witnessed. This is mental. *Merde alors.* Deneuve looks at the girl's red eyes.

What do you want?

Want to be in the same room with him.

I admire your clarity.

Gottago.

After the door closes Deneuve moves all the books on one side of her desk to the other side. Then back. Smell of girl in the room fades slowly.

hommes

Sokrates died in jail. Sappho died in a leap off the white rock of Leukas (for love) so they say. Sokrates is ironical about two things. His beauty (which he calls ugliness) and his knowledge (ignorance). For Sappho irony is a verb. It places her in a certain relation to her own life. How very interesting (Deneuve thinks) to watch myself construct this silk and bitter relation. Latin rhetoricians translate the Greek word *eironia* as *dissimulatio* which means "mask." After all why study the past? Because you may wish to repeat it. And in time (Sappho notes) one's mask becomes one's face. Just before going to jail Sokrates had a conversation with his prosecutors about irony, for this was the real source of their unease, and as he spoke they saw a miniature smoke of grief climb his throat to escape into the room, turning dark now and sulfurous in the confused ash of evening, in the drifting ash alone. *You're a real man Sokrates,* says Deneuve. Closes her notebook. Pulls on her coat and buttons it. *But then so am I.*

je tourne

Poor idea this girl fantasy, Deneuve is thinking as she packs up after the Friday seminar. Girl has missed the last three assignments, will certainly fail the midterm. Deneuve is ducking out the main door onto the street when unexpectedness stumbles in. Girl thrusts some pages at her chest. *Glad I caught you,* she says. Deneuve pulls away. Folds the pages twice. Pushes them down in her briefcase. They circle one another in the doorway. Girl is looking at her oddly.

Never saw you in this state before.

What state is that?

Tonguetied, the girl grins.

Deneuve has a sense of being flicked on a hook. Girl starts to talk about her love in Paris. Who thinks her too dependent. *You?* Deneuve says, hitting the bottom of a volcanic pipe at top speed, all her diamonds going the wrong way. *Toujours comme ça.* Beauty departs. Later at home Deneuve sits by a window. Smell of night so different than smell of day. Frozen darkness like old tin. Like cold cats. Like the word *pauvre.*

nuits

Questions are not all tricks, are they? Deneuve gives a dinner party for the seminar students. She cooks all day. Aubergines shine on the counter. Lettuce fills the sink. Meats drip. Little whites, little blues, the hotel room now replaced by a secluded avenue of the Bois de Bologne. *I know this is hardly your world, are you bored. No I'm not bored.* A girl looks up, blows smoke, grins. This is mental. Night comes. Students arrive. Pile up plates of food. Pour glasses of wine and sit on the floor and say miraculous things. She watches each one. She waits. She sips. Night moves on its way. Food is all over the room, then gradually disappears. Students gather and separate in different doorways, they too gradually disappear. It is almost 2 a.m. when she closes the door, switches off the porchlight, returns slowly along the hall. Out the window she can see snow flying diagonally under a yellow streetlamp. God's punishment, no probably not. Funny it hadn't occurred to her the girl just wouldn't show up. Deneuve drains a wineglass and wipes her mouth. Begins picking up cups and plates and odd bits of food. Puts away chairs. Lines up bottles beside the door. Loads the dishwasher and sits down to watch the rest of the night go by. Hotel room is blowing with moonlight, streaming with moonlight. *What's that you've got there a scar?*

guerres

Weaponry is the topic on Monday. Girl flashes into the seminar twenty minutes late and sits on her left, shirt half tucked in and half out. Deneuve is discussing hoplite armor. Class is sleepy. Text is a poem from the seventh century B.C. about a big room where men store arms. Plumes nod mutely from helmets nailed to roofbeams. Greaves glitter on pegs on the wall. Tunics and hollow shields lie heaped on the floor beside breastplates and belts and Chalcidian swords. *Why is the poet telling us this?* Deneuve asks. No one answers. Not a bee buzzes. Haunted old phrases stare up at them from the book. *What*—she begins but the girl interrupts. *It's about a war not happening.* Deneuve turns. *That's right,* she says. *Nothing is happening.* Bell rings. She leaves the room without looking back.

détails

All the same there are some small questions one would like to put to Sokrates. Or better still Sappho. *Avec tes mains brûlées.*

je traduis

New light is flooding the office when Deneuve arrives Friday. A note is stuck under her door. From a boy who can't come to seminar today *But can I see you at 5 p.m.* scrawled on a page torn out of *Der Spiegel.* Here is Ingeborg Bachmann playing chess. Deneuve studies Ingeborg Bachmann whose clear gaze falls straight down on the little knight at the center of her gameboard, whose shiny bangs are swept by hand to the left. Due to strengthening thoughts of Ingeborg Bachmann's bangs, Deneuve is able to conduct an allusive and slightly sarcastic seminar at top speed on one of her favorite lyric fragments—from the sixth century B.C., a poem about wetness and dryness, about male desire and female desire and how they differ. Imagine a springtime garden of watered boughs and uncut girls. Time holds them deep in its amorous pinch, soaked buds of pure use as female clockwork goes. But what is this black thing that comes parching down like lightning from Thrace with no season or reason—male desire is gears gone mad anywhere anytime without warning or water it shatters the poor poet's lungs! Deneuve pauses. Looks around. No one is asleep. She reads the last verse of the poem aloud. "Lungs" stands in manly exposure as its final word—she repeats this word. Ancient Greek *phrenes.* Usually rendered as "heart" in modern translations because we don't understand very much about how love works. To breathe is to love. She adds a short summary of ancient respiratory theory, avoiding the gaze of the girl who today is seated directly across the table from her, wearing a new earring. *Thank you*, she says after the girl translates a Greek phrase with extreme vulgarity, making the others laugh. Bell rings. Girl leaves abruptly. Deneuve sits quiet as the room empties. Then puts her head down on the table and laughs. How lungs work. As Sappho says:

> To stop breathing is bad.
> So the gods judge.
> For they do not stop breathing.

Later Deneuve goes back down the hall. Inside her office the light is bluing, old ice of April unlacing its fast. She turns at the sound of the five o'clock bell. Comes a knock at the door.

EPITAPH: THAW

Little clicks all night in the back lane there blackness
      Goes leaking out the key.
"It twindles," said Father to April on her
      Anvil of deep decree.

FREUD (2nd draft)

If you go to Iowa visit the Raptor Center.

Down a long gravel road

then over slats

to big wooden boxes.

Bend and peer, it's dark in there.

Set of knobby yellow talons big as jumper cables

glows slowly out

from a shelf near the wall and

above these

the godly tucked presence of (say)

a bald eagle

shuts itself.

That shock of white at the top of the dark

is no daystar no bit of annunciation—

it is head.

Eye shifts this way

and back.

Through a screen

eye watches yellow twigs move on wind.

Body does not move, has only one wing.

All guests of the Center are maimed, rapt away

from the narcissism of nature.

Ultimate things are pleasure

said Freud (1914).

Ultimate things are death

said Freud (1937).

Meanwhile (to cite Goethe) one perfect thorn.

. . . .

For all his sadness there were moments it seemed to him
he had only to make some simple movement
(a swimmer's)
and find himself right back on top.

DIRT AND DESIRE: ESSAY ON THE PHENOMENOLOGY OF FEMALE POLLUTION IN ANTIQUITY

Touches

As members of human society, perhaps the most difficult task we face daily is that of touching one another—whether the touch is physical, moral, emotional or imaginary. Contact is crisis. As the anthropologists say, "Every touch is a modified blow."[1] The difficulty presented by any instance of contact is that of violating a fixed boundary, transgressing a closed category where one does not belong. The ancient Greeks seem to have been even more sensitive than we are to such transgressions and to the crucial importance of boundaries, both personal and extrapersonal, as guarantors of human order. Their society developed a complex cultural apparatus, including rituals like supplication, hospitality and gift exchange, which historians and anthropologists are only recently coming to understand as mechanisms for defining and securing the boundaries of everything in the habitable world. Civilization is a function of boundaries.

In such a society, individuals who are regarded as specially lacking in control of their own boundaries, or as possessing special talents and opportunities for confounding the boundaries of others, evoke fear and controlling action from the rest of society. Women are so regarded in ancient Greek society, along with suppliants, strangers, guests and other intruders. But the threat which women pose is not only greater in degree than that presented by other transgressors of boundaries, it is different in kind. "Let a man not clean his skin in water that a woman has washed in. For a hard penalty follows on that for a long time," Hesiod advises.[2] When we focus upon Greek attitudes to and treatment of the female, we see anxiety about boundaries from a particular perspective—that of hygiene, physical and moral. Considerations of pollution, which do not noticeably predominate in other social rituals like gift exchange or supplication, assert themselves when the crises of contact involve relations between male and female. In order to answer the question "Why?" we have to look surprisingly deep beneath the skin of rituals and individuals both.

Female transgression begins in social fact. Woman is a mobile unit, as a man is not, in a society that practices patrilocal marriage (which Greek society is generally agreed to have done). From birth the male citizen has a fixed place in house and city, but the female moves. At marriage a wife is taken not just (and perhaps not at all) into her husband's heart but into his house. This transgression is necessary (to legitimate continuation of the house), dangerous (insofar as the house incorporates a serious and permanent crisis of contact) and creates the context for illicit varieties of female movement, for example, that of the adulteress out of her husband's house, with attendant damage to male property and reputation. The social fact of female mobility presented Greek society with a set of tactical and moral problems that it never quite solved but which it sought to clarify, during the archaic and classical periods, by recourse to pollution beliefs and the code of conduct governing *miasmata* (defilements) in general.[3] To isolate and insulate the female, from society and from itself, was demonstrably the strategy informing many of the notions, conventions and rituals that surrounded female life in the ancient world. I will examine this strategy for its logic and its practice by asking, first, what the ancients meant by "dirt" and why they disliked it; second, what they did with their dirt and their dislike. It will not be possible, for the most part, to distinguish physical from metaphysical, nor concept from cause. But if we look closely at the dilemma posed by female dirt, we will begin to see the outlines of an ideology of powerful effect. It determined the design not only of the ancient wedding ceremony but also of one of the most famous of the poems of Sappho. We will address these in turn. First let us consider the logic of female pollution.

Logics

Physiologically and psychologically women are wet. Hippokrates differentiates male from female as follows:

> The female flourishes more in an environment of water, from things cold and wet and soft, whether food or drink or activities. The male flourishes more in an environment of fire, from dry, hot foods and mode of life.[4]

Aristotle makes a similar distinction and suggests that this difference may arise from the inclination of the fetus of a male embryo to lean to the right, a female to the left, given that "the right side of the body is hotter than the left."[5] But Aristotle goes on to characterize wetness further in terms illuminating for our discussion of women. He tells us that the wet is that which is not bounded by any boundary of its own but can readily be bounded, while the dry is that which is already bounded by a boundary of its own but can with difficulty be bounded.[6] On this reasoning it becomes possible to differentiate woman from man not only as wet from dry but as the unbounded from the bounded, as content from form, as polluted from pure. We will see in due course that these qualities are closely and necessarily related to one another.

The image of woman as a formless content is one made explicit in the philosophers. Plato compares the matter of creation to a mother, describing it as a "receptacle" or "reservoir" which is "shapeless, viewless, all-receiving" and which "takes its form and activation from whatever shapes enter it."[7] Aristotle accords to the male in the act of procreation the role of active agent, contributing "motion" and "formation" while the female provides the "raw material," as when a bed (the child) is made by a carpenter (the father) out of wood (the mother). Man determines the form, woman contributes the matter. We might note also that the so-called Pythagorean Table of Oppositions, cited by Aristotle, aligns "boundary" or "limit" on the same side as "masculine": over against "the unbounded" and "feminine" on the other side.[8]

The assumptions about women that underlie the views of Plato, Aristotle and the Pythagoreans can be traced to the earliest legends of the Greeks. Myth is a logic too. In myth, woman's boundaries are pliant, porous, mutable. Her power to control them is inadequate, her concern for them unreliable. Deformation attends her. She swells, she shrinks, she leaks, she is penetrated, she suffers metamorphoses. The women of mythology regularly lose their form in monstrosity. Io turns into a heifer, Kallisto becomes a bear, Medusa sprouts snakes from her head and Skylla yelping dogs from her waist, the Sirens and the Sphinx accumulate unmatching bestial parts, while Daphne passes into leaf and Pasiphaë into a mechanical cow. The Graiai are three old women who make themselves repellent by sharing one human form amongst them, passing an eye and a tooth back and forth as needed. Salmakis is a nymph who merges her form with that of her lover to produce a bisexual monster named after him, Hermaphroditos. The Hydra generates heads as fast as they can be chopped off. The Amazons (lacking a breast) owe their fearsomeness to the zeal with which they adapt personal form—their own.

At the same time, the women of myth are notorious adaptors of the forms and boundaries of others. They repeatedly open containers which they are told not to open (e.g., Pandora, the daughters of Kekrops,

Danaë) or destroy something placed in a container in their keeping (as Althaia does the psyche of Meleagros). They prove unreliable as containers themselves: both Zeus and Apollo find it necessary to snatch offspring out of a mother's womb and internalize it for safekeeping (as Zeus takes Dionysos from Semele, Apollo rescues Asklepios from Koronis), while Kronos swallows his children alive as soon as they emerge from Rhea.[9] Even more distressing are the numerous women of myth who submit masculine form to direct and violent reform. Skylla clips a vital lock from her father's head, Agave beheads her son with her bare hands, Medea pulls the plug on Talos, Kybele unmans Attis with an axe. Mythical women frequently violate masculinity by enveloping male form in a fatal formlessness, as Euripides' Klytemnestra encloses Agamemnon in a "garment that has no boundaries"; as Sophokles' Deianira covers Herakles in a "vapor of death" that eats the form of his flesh; as Pindar's Nephele entraps Ixion in the delusion of her own body:

He lay with a cloud—sweet lie![10]

Love is the principal motivation in these stories for women's flight from form or tampering with boundaries. Indeed, the goddess of love, Aphrodite herself, is said to have been born from the earliest recorded revision contrived for manly form by any mythical Greek woman, the castration of Ouranos. To the typical crime of women Greek myth assigns a stereotypical punishment in the legend of the daughters of Danaos: here are forty-nine brides who murder their bridegrooms on their wedding night and are therefore condemned to spend eternity in the underworld gathering water in a sieve or leaky jar.[11] The sieve is a utensil that we will encounter more than once in our investigation of female symbology; for the present, it is enough to say that the sieve of the Danaids sums up in a single hellish image all that is problematic in the relation between women and boundaries.[12]

There is, then, a mythological groundwork of assumptions, also operative in the arguments of philosophers like Plato and Aristotle and which can be related to historical behavior, that regards women as formless creatures who cannot or do not or will not maintain their own boundaries and who are awfully adept at confounding the boundaries of others. When we begin to look for the etiology of this conception, we encounter, I believe, a deep and abiding mistrust of "the wet" in virtue of its ability to transform and deform.

For it is the consensus of Greek thought that the soundest condition for a human being is dryness, provided it is not excessive dryness. "A dry soul is wisest and best," Heraklitos asserts. Mature men in a sound and unafflicted condition are dry—for example, Zeus, whose efficiently functioning mind is characterized as "dry lungs" by Homer. Wetness of mind is an intellectually deficient condition; so Aristophanes speaks of a man's need to "dry his mind" if he wants to "say anything smart," while Heraklitos ascribes to a "wet psyche" the inability of a drunk to find his way home. The dry state of mental alertness can be undermined in various ways. Diogenes of Apollonia proposed in the fifth century that the conscious element in man consists of air and that an individual's intelligence depends on the dryness of this air:

Understanding is the work of the pure and dry air. For moisture hinders intelligence, wherefore in sleep and in drunkenness and in surfeit, understanding is diminished.[13]

The assault of emotion is also regarded by ancient authors as an endangering wetness. Emotion is a liquid or liquefying substance that pours into a person and dissolves him. Fear is "wet" in Archilochos and causes

Anakreon to "drizzle." Anxiety "falls in drops" within the minds of a Greek tragic chorus. Envy melts the eyes and heart of the envious in a Hellenistic epigram.[14] Of all the emotions, by far the most devastating are those of erotic desire, for love combines a liquescent effect with fiery heat: the lover who is not melted away by Eros is likely to be burned to a crisp. Thus desire is variously said to melt, flood, soften, loosen, boil, broil, roast, drown and disintegrate the lover who is his victim.[15] Men pride themselves on being able to resist such assaults on their physiological and psychological boundaries. A fragment of Sophokles instructs us, "The chest of a good man does not soften." Ancient medical theory endorses the view that dryness is best and is a masculine prerogative. According to Hippokrates, the maturity of the male physique is achieved when the element of fire within "steadies itself" and the body "no longer trembles with growth" but rather attains and keeps its proper dry form.[16]

Wantons

This condition of dry stability is never attained by the female physique, which presumably remains cold and wet all its life[17] and so more subject than the male to liquefying assaults upon body and mind, especially those of emotion. That the female is softer than the male and much more easily moved to tears, pity, jealousy, despondency, fear, rash impulses and sexual desire is a *communis opinio* of ancient literature, voiced by such widely differing temperaments as Aristotle, Empedokles and Semonides of Amorgos.[18] Throughout these sources, greatest attention is given to the emotions of love. Women are assumed to be markedly more open to erotic desire than men and sexually insatiable once aroused. A long tradition concerning female lechery derives from this assumption, of which a few examples may be mentioned. Aeschylus warns against the "blazing eye" of a woman who has once "tasted man" and deprecates female license as "ready to dare anything" for love. Sophokles observes that even women who have sworn to avoid the pain of childbirth cannot resist sexual desire. The lust of women is a frequent joke in Aristophanes. Alkiphron characterizes female sexual voracity as a "Charybdis," warning another man that his *hetaira* will swallow him whole. Both Hippokrates and Plato promote the theory of the "wandering womb," an explanation of feminine hysteria which is posited upon women's uncontrollable longing for sex. Aristotle takes female depravity for granted as a consequence of feminine weakness and a reason for marrying girls off not later than the age of eighteen.[19] In the Greek historians, whenever mention is made of a society or state of affairs managed by women, it is assumed that such situations would feature total female promiscuity. For example, Philo of Byblos, accounting for traditions of matrilinear descent in antiquity, explains: "They traced their descent on the mother's side because women at that time had intercourse casually with any man they ran into." Philo takes it for granted that, unrestrained by an alternate system, women would incline to complete wantonness.[20]

What is the connection between wantonness and wetness? First, their moisture and malleability make women more vulnerable to the onslaughts of erotic desire upon psychic form. Second, female wetness gives women a weapon, which men do not possess, against the excessive heat and dryness that may accompany desire. Hippokrates maintains that the parching heat of the Dog Days (late July) is beneficial for those "phlegmatic by nature," a class which includes "women and watery men," but it causes the generality of men to "wither right up." Aristotle pursues this matter in an erotic direction; he asks, "Why are men less capable of sexual intercourse in summer but women more so?" and answers:

....

Because hot natures collapse in summer by excess of heat, while cold ones flourish. Now a man is hot and dry but a woman is cold and moist. So the power of a man is diminished at that time but a woman's power flourishes because it is balanced by its contrary.[21]

We find in poetry too this concern for the withering effect of the Dog Days upon masculine physique. Alkaios of Lesbos, a lyric poet of the seventh century B.C., represents the time of the rising of Sirios as a season of blistering heat which parches men to incapacity while encouraging the license of women to flourish.[22] As the poem shifts from weather to physiology, it becomes clear that the focus of masculine concern (and perhaps resentment) is not a summer heatwave but the unwitherable appetite and capacity of the female sex:

> Wet your lungs with wine for the star is coming round.
> The season is harsh, all things thirst beneath the heat.
> From the leaves the cricket sends sweet noise,
> pouring down from its wings
> one shrill song after another,
> when in blazing summer . . .
> the artichoke blooms. And now is the time
> when women are at their most polluted
> but men are delicate, for the Dog Star
> parches head and knees. . . .

One word here calls for particular attention. Editors of Alkaios generally caution us that we cannot know exactly what the poet means by μιαρώτατι: "most polluted." Translators are inclined to reduce the word to a term of nonspecific abuse like "abominable" or "accursed." To judge from the rest of his poetry, however, Alkaios' vocabulary of abuse is anything but nonspecific; he is one of the most outspoken blame poets of the archaic period. Moreover, a powerful clue to his meaning can be read from a few verses of the Boeotian poet Hesiod. For Alkaios has clearly modelled his own poem on a well-known section of Hesiod's *Works and Days*.[23] In almost identical terms Hesiod describes a midsummer scene where artichokes bloom, crickets pour forth song after song, goats are rich and fat, wine is perfect. Then he adds:

> . . . And women are at their most lecherous (μαχλόταται)
> while men are completely enfeebled.

Both poets agree on the physics of the situation: men are parched to impotence by the heat; women seem somehow to thrive in it, encouraged to burgeon as wantonly as flora and fauna. In another passage Hesiod states this case more openly (in the midst of giving advice on how to choose a wife):

> For a man wins no better prize than a good
> woman, and none more chilling than a bad one—
> always hunting something to devour.
> And no matter how strong he is,
> she roasts her man without fire,
> and hands him over to a raw old age.[24]

Hesiod here abandons metaphors of weather and identifies the withering factor as female sexual power itself. The voracious woman, by her unending demands, "roasts her man" in the unquenchable fire of her appetite, drains his manly strength and delivers him to the "raw old age" of premature impotence.[25] We find a similar complaint in the Alexandrian poet Palladas:

> Woman is the wrath of Zeus, a gift given in place of fire
>> cruel countergift!
> For she burns a man with cares and withers him up
>> and brings old age on youth too soon.[26]

And the archaic poet Archilochos summarizes the female threat in two iambic verses:

> She came carrying water in one hand
> the tricky-minded female, and fire in the other.[27]

These Greek poets find sexuality in women a fearsome thing.[28] It threatens the very essence of a man's manliness and its foundations are cosmic. United by a vital liquidity with the elemental world, woman is able to tap the inexhaustible reservoirs of nature's procreative power. Man, meanwhile, holds himself fiercely and thoughtfully apart from this world of plants, animals and female wantonness—doubly estranged from it, by his inherent dryness of form and by the masculine virtue of self-control ($\sigma\omega\phi\rho\sigma\nu\eta$)[29] with which he maintains form. The unfailing moisture and sexual drive of woman, then, is part of a larger conceptual schema, whereby the female is assimilated to the world of raw nature and femininity insistently identified with the wild. "Woman is one great bestiality!" Menander says. Ancient classical culture was neither the first nor the last to subscribe to this notion; what is important for our purpose is to see where the notion led. The words of a later author, the second-century sophist Aelian, give some indication. In his treatise *On the Nature of Animals* Aelian concludes his discussion of poisonous vipers by telling us that the asp is the most poisonous of all. Then he adds, "But a wild animal even more polluted [μιαρώτερον] than an asp is the woman who dabbles in poisons."[30] The force of Aelian's designation "more polluted" here clearly depends on collapsing the categories of female and animal.

Beasts

The notion of female wildness, current in Greek thinking from prehistoric right through classical times, is a coin with two sides. The presexual female appears in literature as an untamed animal who prefers, given a choice, to live the wild life of Artemis, roaming the woods undomesticated and unloving of men. She is called "rather wild" or "unbroken" or "unused by the bull" and is characterized as a fawn, a heifer, a filly, a snake, a gazelle, an unfledged bird, a swelling bean, a ripening apple. The sexually initiated woman, on the other hand, unless she enjoys the benefits of masculine supervision, soon proceeds from licentiousness to bestialization. The mature and sexually active female is thus referred to as a bitch, an ass, a weasel, a brood mare and a wild sow pawing to be loosed. The word *hippos* (horse) is a well-known Greek idiom for "lecherous woman." Aristotle explains why: "In eagerness for sexual intercourse, of all female animals the mare comes first, next the cow. Mares become horse-mad and the term derived from this one animal is applied by way of abuse to women who are inordinate in their sexual desires."[31]

More than idiomatic consequences follow, however, from classifying woman with the wilderness. We are told that Themistokles once yoked four prostitutes to a chariot and drove them into the marketplace.[32] It is by the way we classify one another that we shape our moral expectations, of one another and of ourselves. The Greek female was expected to be no more in command of herself or her impulses than a bitch in heat.[33] This conviction was given early expression in the legislation of Solon, which restricted the walks, feasts, trousseaux, mourning, food, drink and sexual activity of women, and also later by the institution of the *gynaikonomoi* (supervisors of women), special magistrates appointed to maintain feminine "decency" or "good order."[34] Solon's legislation is but one well-publicized example of a complex array of restrictions on the movements and attire and actions of woman, on the spaces and gestures and garments within which she lived. A similar resolve informs all these restrictions: since woman does not bound herself, she must *be bounded.* The celebrated Greek virtue of self-control (*sophrosyne*) has to be defined differently for men and for women, Aristotle maintains. Masculine *sophrosyne* is rational self-control and resistance to excess, but for the woman *sophrosyne* means obedience and consists in submitting herself to the control of others.[35]

In her natural state, then, woman demands the attention of culture to impose those boundaries, physical and metaphysical, that will guarantee her virtue against transgression and digression. Xenophon describes the women's quarters of a typical fifth-century house as "set off from the men's quarters by a bolted door so that nothing could be carried off from inside which should not be carried off and so that the male servants might not beget children without our knowledge."[36] Xenophon's terms are ambiguous. He does not tell us on which side the bolted door was bolted: the pregnability of female boundaries presents male culture with a problem that has more than two sides. Woman is subject not only to incursion from without but to leakage from within and, for this reason, her very presence may pose a threat to the integrity of the house of which she is a part and the city that encompasses it. For this reason, Athenian law forbade a husband who had caught his wife in adultery to continue living in the same house with her. For this reason, women guilty of adultery were debarred by law from the public sacrifices. And this exclusion was necessary, Demosthenes explains, "in order that there not be pollutions nor sacrileges in holy places."[37] In order to see exactly what Demosthenes means by "pollutions" here, we have to take seriously the topography of sacred and profane. Adulteresses pose a spatial threat to the public hygiene of his city. Their dirt is something they carry with them like a contagion. Which brings us to the question "What is dirt?"

Dirts

"Dirt" may be defined as "matter out of place." The poached egg on your plate at breakfast is not dirt; the poached egg on the floor of the Reading Room of the British Museum is. Dirt is matter that has crossed a boundary it ought not to have crossed. Dirt confounds categories and mixes up form. Robert Parker's study of *miasma* emphasizes that this word has in Greek the basic sense "defilement" or "impairment of a thing's integrity."[38] But dirt is not passive. Mary Douglas calls pollution "a particular class of dangers which are not powers vested in humans but which can be released by human action."[39] Women, then, are pollutable, polluted and polluting in several ways at once. They are anomalous members of the human class, being, as Aristotle puts it, imperfect men. They are as individuals comparatively formless themselves, without firm control of personal boundaries. They are, as social entities, units of danger, moving across boundaries of family and house, in marriage, prostitution, or adultery. They are, as psychological entities, unstable compounds of deceit and desire, prone to leakage.

In sum, the female body, the female psyche, the female social life and the female moral life are penetrable, porous, mutable and subject to defilement all the time. So when Aelian labels a woman "a wild animal more polluted than an asp," he goes on to explain that "an asp destroys with its poison but a woman has only to touch her victim to kill it." The female touch is a deadly crisis: her pollution leaks out at the slightest contact. A house or a society that did not take adequate measures to contain the leakage of its women could be said to be sailing the sea of life in a Melian boat, according to ancient proverbial wisdom. The expression "Melian boat," connoting a proverbially leaky vessel, first arose in connection with a certain Hippotes who was designated to found a colony for the Melians. But the Melian men refused to sail with him. "They made excuses, some saying that their boats were leaking, others that their wives were unwell, and so they stayed home. Hippotes then laid a curse on them: that they should never find a boat that was water-tight, and that they should be ruled by women forever."[40] Hippotes' curse is one aimed at the very fabric and common sense of Melian life. Woman out of control is the danger, a boat filled with holes is its image. Hippotes is condemning Melian civilization to chaos.

Leaks

We find this same metaphor, deployed from the feminine point of view, in a poem of Sappho's, apparently composed during her exile in Sicily, in which she characterizes the chaos of everyday life in exile as "leakage" and represents it as an emergency for female boundaries:

(a)   . . . for my mother [used to say that]
           in her youth, if someone had her hair tied round
           with a purple band
           this was a great ornament indeed.
           But the girl with hair yellower
           than a flame . . .

             [suitable for] crowns
        of richblooming flowers. . . .
             Now just recently

        from Sardis a brightcolored headbinder . . .
             . . . [cities] . . .

(b)   For you, Kleis,

           I have no idea where I can get
           a brightcolored headbinder.
           But as for the Mytilenean one. . . .

                        . . .

           I had . . .
                   brightcolored . . .

           these things of the Kleanaktidai . . .
           exile . . . [city]
                   memories:

                   . . . terribly leaked away. . . .[41]

Damaged though the text is, we can see it is a poem about matter out
of place, a lament from exile. Sappho regrets the loss of her city and of
the order of life she had known there as something "terribly leaked
away," in the final verse of the fragment. But throughout the earlier
verses that loss is symbolized as absence of female headbinder. This item
of apparel, which Sappho wishes to obtain for her daughter, Kleis, is
evidently unavailable in Sicily, although in the good old days in Myti-

....

lene, Sappho's mother used to talk about proper techniques for binding the hair and would presumably have seen to it that Kleis got what a girl needs. Exile entails the frustration of such needs and a dislocation of the style of life that depends on them.

Sappho uses the word κόσμος (in verse 3 of the Greek text) to designate this misplaced style of life and the headbinder that represents it. *Kosmos*, here translated "ornament," implies in Greek all kinds of "good order," from the arrangement of planets in the sky to the style with which an individual wears her hat. In the language of politics, *kosmos* means the constitution or good government of a city. In the language of cosmology, *kosmos* means the entire, perfect, ordered universe. According to one ancient cosmology, cosmos was first assembled out of chaos, when Zeus threw a veil over the head of the goddess of the underworld, Chthonie, and married her. So Pherekydes tells us and he goes on to describe the veil, on which were embroidered earth, ocean and the houses of ocean—that is to say, the contours of the civilized world. Once veiled by her bridegroom, the dark and formless chthonic goddess was transformed and renamed Ge, goddess of the visible world, decorous and productive wife of Zeus.[42]

I call attention to the cosmology of Pherekydes because it concerns the wedding of Zeus. Ancient wedding ceremonies are one place where the theory of female pollution and the practice of pollution control can be seen to converge. Pherekydes introduces us directly, as Sappho did obliquely, to the vestiary code that regulates female decency in the ancient world and informs the sacred symbolism of the marriage rite. The head is its focus. Headgear is crucial to female honor, an index of sexual purity and civilized status.[43] No decent woman is seen in public without her headdress; only children, prostitutes and maenads run about unveiled. The most common Greek word for female headgear is *kredemnon*, whose symbolic force can be read from its threefold usage. Properly signifying a woman's headbinder, *kredemnon* is also used to mean "battlements of a city" and "stopper of a bottle."[44] It is plain what these three have in common. A corked bottle, a fortified city, a veiled woman, are vessels whose contents are sealed against dirt and loss. To put the lid on certifies purity.

Lids

Putting the lid on female purity was the chief concern and ritual point of the ancient wedding ceremony.[45] So in the cosmology of Pherekydes, Zeus marries the goddess of the underworld by bestowing upon her a cosmic map of her own proper boundaries. So also, in the Athenian legend of the invention of marriage by Kekrops, we see masculine clarity and control imposed on a chaos of female promiscuity.[46] For we are told that Kekrops "found men and women having intercourse at random, so that no son could tell who his father was, no father who was his son." Kekrops accordingly devised the institution of marriage, to put an end to sexual license and clarify the lines of patrilineal descent; for this service he came to be regarded as a culture hero, who led the Athenians "out of savagery into civilization."[47] So too, in historical time, we find Plutarch describing the Boeotian wedding ceremony in these terms:

> After veiling the bride they put on her head a crown of asparagus, for this plant yields the sweetest fruit from the harshest thorns and so may the bride, if properly managed, provide a civilized and sweet contribution to her husband's life despite her original roughness and sourness.[48]

The ancient wedding ritual undertook, systematically, to redeem woman from her original roughness and sourness and to purify her of

chaos by means of certain very specific ceremonies aimed at the drama-
tization and reinforcement of female boundaries. So we find in the
marriage rite much emphasis on doorways, thresholds, lintels, exits,
entrances and the whole ceremonial apparatus whereby the bride is relo-
cated from her father's house to her husband's house, from maidenhood
to married status. The wedding so conceived, as a rite of passage
between households, has been the subject of much study by historians,
anthropologists and others. But I think we can better articulate the
meaning of this rite if we pay attention not so much to the boundaries of
houses as to the boundaries of the bride herself and insist upon one spe-
cial moment in the ceremony—the climax of the whole proceeding, the
moment when pollution danger is most acute and ritual counterstrategy
most outspoken.

The ancient wedding begins in the house of the bride's father, with
preliminary rites carried out by the bride, including a formal farewell to
her girlhood and nuptial bath. After the bath she is dressed in wedding
attire and veiled in a veil that must cover her face. Sacrifices are offered
to the divinities of marriage (Zeus Teleios, Hera Teleia, Aphrodite,
Artemis, Peitho) and then a feast is spread where all the wedding guests
share with the bride her last meal in her father's house. During this feast
the women all sit together on a special couch on the right side of the
doorway, facing the men who sit together on the left of the door. At some
point in the feasting, a child wearing a crown of thorns goes among
the guests offering bread from a sieve and repeating the formula "I
have fled evil, I have found what is better."[49] This action, which prefig-
ures the climax of the ceremony, deserves attention. The verbal formula
is one known to us from the mystery rituals where it was uttered by the
initiate after his lustration, symbolizing a final separating out of evil
from good. In the nuptial context these words signify, so Zenobios tells
us, that "the bridal couple are to thrust off their former wild ways and

find a civilized living."[50] The thorny and savage bride, then, is about to be salvaged for civilization by the nuptial function. And that redeeming function is represented in the relation between leaky vessel (the sieve in which bread is carried) and the good gift of bread itself which ritual calls forth from the leaky vessel. It is important to note that throughout the feasting and the distribution of bread the bride remains very strictly veiled, for it is not until the end of all these events that the climax of the ceremony occurs: this is the moment when the bride rises or turns in her place and, facing her bridegroom and the men of his household across the room, takes off her veil.

A red-figure loutrophoros in the Boston Museum of Fine Arts depicts this moment in the wedding.[51] Here we see the bride facing her bridegroom, who watches her intently as she lifts the veil from her head, assisted by a female attendant (*nympheutria*) standing behind her.[52] This action, called the *anakalypteria* (unveiling), gives its name to the whole first stage of the ceremony. It signifies official consecration of the marriage so that, from this moment, the bride is considered to *be married*.[53] The elaborate gifts given by the bridegroom to the bride at this stage of the wedding were called *ta anakalypteria*, "unveiling gifts"; but they had an alternate name, *ta diaparthenia* (virginity gifts) and were so called, Pollux tells us, because they were regarded as "gifts given in exchange for taking away the virginity of the bride."[54]

In other words, as far as the bride is concerned, the *anakalypteria* is the decisive sacral action of the wedding. At the moment of unveiling, for the first time, the intact boundary of her person is violated by contact: the contact of vision. Ancient lexical sources leave no doubt that visual exposure was the function and official point of the ritual of the *anakalypteria*. "In order that she may be seen by the men" is the reason why the bride unveils herself, the lexicographers tell us.[55] Once she has done so, the glance of the bridegroom from across the room penetrates her opened veil. She is no longer *parthenos*. She is touched.

This is the moment referred to, metonymically, by Pherekydes in his account of the sacred marriage of Zeus and Chthonie, for he concludes his description of their wedding by saying: "People allege that this was the first *anakalypteria* and from this arose the custom for gods and men."[56] This is the moment renounced by Andromache in Homer's *Iliad* when, upon hearing of Hektor's death, she takes hold of the *kredemnon* on her head (a wedding gift from Aphrodite) and hurls it to the ground.[57] This is the moment exposed (or overexposed) by Sappho in perhaps the most controversial of her poems:

> He seems to me equal to gods that man
> who opposite you
> sits and listens close
> to your sweet speaking
>
> and lovely laughing—oh it
> puts the heart in my chest on wings
> for when I look at you, a moment, then no speaking
> is left in me
>
> no: tongue breaks and thin
> fire is racing under skin
> and in eyes no sight and drumming
> fills ears
>
> and cold sweat holds me and shaking
> grips me all, greener than grass
> I am and dead—or almost
> I seem to me. . . . [58]

Let us entertain the hypothesis that Sappho's lyric strategy in this poem is to insert us imaginatively into the ritual moment of the *anakalypteria*; that the man in the poem represents a bridegroom observing his bride at the moment of her unveiling; and that Sappho has projected herself into the role of the *nympheutria* who (as illustrated in the red-figure vase mentioned above) stands behind the bride and helps her unveil.[59] Considered in this light, some of the poem's notorious oddities clarify themselves. For example, the unnamed man who appears in verse 1 only to disappear in verse 2 does so because this is the moment in the wedding ritual which, although contingent upon the presence of the groom, belongs more than any other to the bride. The man is the initial subject and visual focus of the poem because Sappho, if positioned behind the bride's back, is looking straight at him over the bride's head. For the same reason, namely her rearguard position, Sappho does not at first respond to what the bride looks like, since she cannot see her face, but rather to the bride's voice and laughter, which she is well positioned to hear. The contrast that follows, however, between the bridegroom and Sappho is framed in visual terms ("when I look at you") to emphasize and exploit the basic ritual fiction of the moment, the fiction that at the *anakalypteria* the bridegroom is seeing his bride unveiled for the first time, whereas Sappho has evidently seen the girl numerous times before and yet cannot accommodate herself to the vision.

The poem is framed in verbs of seeming. "He seems to me" (*phainetai*) it begins. "I seem to me" (*phainomai*) it ends. The Greek verb φαίνεσθαι means "to be seen," "to appear," "to be made manifest," "to stand revealed." As a confession of love and at the same time an evocation of the *anakalypteria*, this is a poem devised "out of revelation itself," as Longinus says. Yet it is not the bride who stands revealed at this wedding. It is not the material boundaries of a bridal veil that fall open. It is not the bridegroom who suddenly sees what he has not seen before. Sappho has constructed her poem as a play upon the ritual formalities of the unveiling ceremony in order to situate her own emotions, which are intensely personal and properly hidden emotions, at the single most extraordinary moment of exposure in female life and so to bend its ritual meaning onto herself with an irony of reference as sharp as a ray of light. The result is what James Joyce would call "infrahuman": the bride is unveiled, but the poet renders herself transparent. And, in a strange way, Sappho's poem confirms everything we have been listening to the Greeks say about the female, namely that she plays havoc with boundaries and defies the rules that keep matter in its place. I suppose this is deliberate. Sappho has chosen the most solemn and authoritative of the rituals that sacralize female boundaries and used it to explode the distinction between the outside and the inside of her self. In the end I am not sure we can precisely define the spirit in which she does so. Sappho is one of those people of whom the more you see the less you know. But it might well have been for Sappho, as representative of the whole mysterious, polluted species of ancient womanhood, that Dorothy Parker composed her famous epitaph:

If you can read this, you've come too close.

1. E. Crawley, *The Mystic Rose* (New York 1927), I. 78.

2. Hesiod, *Works and Days,* 753–5.

3. Many societies resort to codes of pollution to regulate and rationalize human situations where order and sense elude them, like sex. "When moral rules are obscure or contradictory there is a tendency for pollution beliefs to simplify or clarify the point at issue," says Mary Douglas, *Purity and Danger: An Analysis of Concepts of Pollution and Taboo* (London 1966), 141. See also R. Parker, *Miasma: Pollution and Purification in Early Greek Religion* (Oxford 1983).

4. Hippokrates, *On Regimen,* 27.

5. Aristotle, *Problems,* 879a33–34; cf. 88a12–20; *Generation of Animals,* 765b2.

6. Aristotle, *On Generation and Corruption,* 329b31–33.

7. Plato, *Timaeus,* 49a; 50b–d.

8. Aristotle, *Generation of Animals,* 716a6–7; 727b31–34; 729b15–21; *Physics* 192a20–25; *Metaphysics* 986a22–30.

9. Rhea's name is pertinent, derived from the verb ῥεῖν: "to flow," "to stream," "to pour," "to gush out."

10. Euripides, *Orestes,* 25; Sophokles, *Trachiniai,* 831; Pindar, *Pythians,* 2.36–37.

11. On the Danaids, see the survey by A. F. Garvie, *Aeschylus' Supplices: Play and Trilogy* (Cambridge 1969), 234–5.

12. The image of woman as a sieve furnishes Aristophanes (*Ekklesiazousai,* 991) with a joke that is mainly misconstrued by commentators: a young man wards off the sexual advances of an old woman with the words "Well, at the moment it's not a sieve I want!" Surely this is not a reference to the older woman's flour-whitened face or floury-white hair but implies that a lifetime of sexual experience has not enhanced her desirability.

13. Heraklitos, fr. B118 Diels; Homer, *Iliad,* 14.165; Aristophanes, *Knights,* 95–96; cf. *Wasps,* 1452; Heraklitos, fr. B117 Diels; Diogenes of Apollonia, fr. A19 Diels. Kritias says that, in drunkenness, memory is melted out of the mind by forgetfulness and the mind trips (fr. B6.12 Diels).

14. Archilochos, fr. 122.4 West; Anakreon, fr. 395.4 *PMG;* Aeschylus, *Agamemnon,* 179–80; *Palatine Anthology,* 11.193.

15. In the absence of any satisfactory etymology for the Greek ἐράω (I desire) applied to one moved sexually, Onians suggests an original derivation from ἐράω (I pour

out) related to ἔρσα (dew) and signifying in the middle voice "I pour myself out, emit liquid, am poured out." He compares στυγέω (I hate), which began in the physical "I freeze, stiffen at": R. B. Onians, *The Origins of European Thinking about the Body, the Mind, the Soul, the World, Time and Fate* (Cambridge 1951), 202 n.4.

16. Sophokles, fr. 195 Pearson; Hippokrates, *On Regimen*, 33.

17. Cf. Aristotle, *Generation of Animals*, 728a19–22; *Problems*, 879a.

18. Aristotle, *History of Animals*, 608b; Empedokles, fr. B62.1 Diels; Semonides, fr. 7 West.

19. Aeschylus, fr. 243 Nauck; *Choephoroi*, 594; Sophokles, fr. 932 Pearson; Aristophanes, *Thesmophoriazousai*, 504ff; *Knights*, 468–70; 616–20; *Lysistrata*, 553–9; Alkiphron, 1.6.2; 3.33; Hippokrates, *Diseases of Women*, 1; Plato, *Timaeus*, 91c; Aristotle, *Nicomachean Ethics*, 1150b6; *Politics*, 1335a29.

20. Simon Pembroke discusses a tendency on the part of Greek writers to identify matriarchal situations with female promiscuity on the basis of little evidence, no evidence, or in the face of contradictory evidence and persuades us that such stories were contrived not so much to verify that a matriarchal state of affairs ever existed but rather to show how awful life would have been if it had: "Women in Charge: the Function of Alternatives in Early Greek Tradition and the Ancient Idea of Matriarchy," *Journal of the Courtald and Warburg Institutes* 30 (1967): 1–35. See also S. Pembroke, "Last of the Matriarchs," *Journal of the Economic and Social History of the Orient* 8 (1965); P. Vidal-Naquet, "Esclavage et gynécocratie dans la tradition, le mythe, l'utopie," *Recherches sur les structures sociales dans l'antiquité classique* (Paris 1970).

21. Hippokrates, *Airs Waters Places*, 10.85ff; Aristotle, *Problems*, 879a31–35.

22. Alkaios, fr. Z23 Page.

23. Hesiod, *Works and Days*, 582–96.

24. Ibid., 702–5.

25. See also ibid., 700–5; and cf. *Othello:* "O curse of marriage, that we can call / These delicate creatures ours / And not their appetites!" (III.3.268).

26. *Palatine Anthology*, 9.165.1–4; cf. Hesiod, *Works and Days*, 57.

27. Archilochos, fr. 184 West.

28. A man and woman in Theokritos debate this fear: *Idylls*, 27.27–28.

29. Helen North, *Sophrosyne: Self-Knowledge and Self-Restraint in Greek Literature* (Ithaca 1966), and below.

....

30. Menander, fr. 488 Kock; Aelian, *On the Nature of Animals,* 1.54; cf. Lucretius, *De Rerum Natura,* 6.17–23.

31. Aristotle, *History of Animals,* 572a8–13.

32. Athenaios, 533d.

33. A bull-struck cow will mount the bull herself, Aristotle warns, no herdsman can check her: *History of Animals,* 572a30–b4.

34. C. Wehrli, "Les gynéconomes," *Museum Helveticum* 19 (1962): 33–38.

35. Aristotle, *Politics* 1260a20–24; 1277b21–25. Cf. Freud in a letter to Eduard Silberstein (January 7, 1919): "A thinking man is his own legislator and confessor, and obtains his own absolution, but the woman, let alone the girl, does not have the measure of ethics in herself. She can only act if she keeps within the limits of morality, following what society has established as fitting. She is never forgiven if she has revolted against morality, possibly rightly so."

36. Xenophon, *Oikonomika,* 9.5.

37. Demosthenes, *Against Neaira,* 59.86.

38. Parker (above, n.3), 3.

39. Douglas (above, n.3), 113.

40. For the Melian proverb, see Photios, *Lexicon,* 594.9; Aristotle, fr. 554 Rose; Simon Pembroke (above, n.20) interprets the proverb as corresponding to the more general stipulation "that the earth shall bear no fruit and the sea shall be impossible to sail" in conventional curses (32). But I think it likely that specific sexual and eugenic anxieties are not far beneath the surface of this story. In a society so "unwell" that wives dictate public policy, what man can navigate the waters of everyday life, what husband can even be sure he is the father of his children? Cf. the Odyssean situation: nineteen years of woman's rule in a house that lets in suitors like a sieve provoke from Telemachos the comment "No one ever knows his own begetting" (*Odyssey,* 1.215; 4. 387; cf. Lysias, *Eratosthenes,* 1.33; Euripides, fr. 1015 Nauck.)

41. Sappho, fr. 98 (a) and (b) Lobel.

42. Pherekydes, fr. 50–54 Diels.

43. Michael Nagler has proposed that the two *amphipoloi* ("attendants" or "ones going on either side") who accompany a respectable woman everywhere (e.g., *Iliad,* 24.90–94; *Odyssey,* 18.182–4) similarly betoken chastity, as if the two attendants were regarded as a surrogate personal boundary. An encircled woman is bounded against contact or leakage. A woman deprived of such encirclement is prey to seizure

....

155

and rape (e.g., *Homeric Hymn to Demeter,* 5; *Homeric Hymn to Aphrodite,* 117; 120; Moschos, *Europa,* 28–32). The decorous Nausikaa even sleeps with a handmaid on either side. When she must confront Odysseus unprotected by veil (cast off at 6.100) or companions (left behind at 6.139), Nausikaa maintains personal boundaries by "holding herself" (*Odyssey,* 6.141). This seems a variation upon the conventional feminine gesture of *aidos,* which is to "hold the veil up in front or on either side of the face" (e.g., *Odyssey,* 18.210). The sham *aidos* of a whore perverts this gesture as it pollutes the veil she wears; a *hetaira* enters the room "holding up to her cheeks her filthy veil": so the parodist Matron, cited by M. Nagler, *Spontaneity and Tradition: A Study in the Oral Art of Homer* (Berkeley 1974), 67 n.5. The association of a decent woman's headgear with her battle against pollution is further implied by the word that Sappho (fr. 110 Lobel) and Hekataios (*FGH,* I.25) use for such covering: *cheiromaktron,* primarily "a cloth for wiping the hands after washing." E. Crawley (above, n.1) discusses the use of veils as protection against infecting others or being infected by evil influences (I.273). Sappho adds that the Graces despise a woman whose head is without a *stephanos* ("crown": fr. 81b Lobel). On the conventional female gesture of holding the veil, see J. Boardman, "Old Smyrna: The Attic Pottery," *British Society of Archaeology* 53–54 (1958–9): 152–81; 159 and pl.9.11; F. Johansen, *Attic Grave Reliefs* (London 1951), 41; F. Studniczka, *Beiträge zür Geschichte der altgriechischen Tracht* (Berlin 1927), 125–6.

44. Homer, *Iliad,* 22.470; 16.100; *Odyssey,* 3.392.

45. Cf. Latin *nubere,* "to marry," probably cognate with *nubes,* "cloud," and meaning literally "to veil oneself" (*Oxford Latin Dictionary,* s.v.).

46. For a useful corrective to the usual anthropological reading of this myth, see C. Patterson, "Attikai: The Other Athenians," *Helios* 13 (1992): 45–62.

47. Scholia on Aristophanes, *Wealth,* 773.

48. Plutarch, *Conjugal Precepts,* 138d. Similarly, we find the bridegroom in Xenophon's *Oikonomika* speaking of his bride as a wild animal which, after the wedding, gradually became "submissive to my hand and domesticated enough to make conversation" (7–10).

49. Zenobios, 3.98–99; E. Samter, *Familienfeste der Griechen und Römer* (Berlin 1901), 99.

50. Zenobios (3.98) goes on to say that this formula became a proverb "applicable to

people who anticipate some change for the better in themselves." On marriage as acculturation, see Vidal-Naquet (above, n.20), 77.

51. J. H. Oakley, "The Anakalypteria," *Archäologischer Anzeiger* 97 (1982): 113–18.

52. The boy standing between the couple can probably be identified as the "child crowned with thorns," mentioned above, who distributes bread from a sieve and repeats the ritual formula of nuptial redemption. No one has yet named the large object suspended over the bridegroom's head: a bread-filled sieve?

53. Sources of information on the *anakalypteria* include the lexical entries for this term in Harpokration, Hesychius, Pollux and Suidas; A. Bruckner "Anakalypteria," *Archäologische Gesellschaft zu Berlin* 64 (1904): 60; M. L. Cunningham, "Aeschylus' *Agamemnon* 231–247," *Bulletin of the Institute for Classical Studies* 31 (1984): 9–12; I. S. Mark, "The Gods on the East Frieze of the Parthenon," *Hesperia* 53 (1984): 291–303; M. E. Mayo, "The Gesture of Anakalypsis," *American Journal of Archaeology* 77 (1973): 210–21; J. H. Oakley (above, n.51); J. Toutain, "Le rite nuptial de l'anakalypterion," *Révue des études archaiques* 42 (1940): 345–53.

54. Pollux, *Onomastikon*, 3.39.

55. Suidas; Harpokration; s.v. *anakalypteria*.

56. Pherekydes, fr. 50 Diels.

57. Homer, *Iliad*, 22.469–73.

58. Sappho, fr. 31 Lobel. Longinus' citation of the poem (*de Sublimitate*, 10) includes a defective and controversial seventeenth verse, but, as critics have noted, verses 1 through 16 appear to constitute a rhythmical and conceptual whole—whether poem or section of a poem. See H. Saake, *Zur Kunst Sapphos* (Paderborn 1971), 35, for full bibliography on the question.

59. The theory (first advanced by Ulrich von Wilamowitz-Moellendorff, *Sappho und Simonides* [Berlin 1913], 58) that fr. 31 was actually performed at a wedding as some kind of *epithalamium* seems incredible. This poem does not participate in the meaning toward which it points, as ritual language must, but tropologizes it. For further bibliography on fr. 34, see E. Robbins, "Every Time I Look at You . . . Sappho Thirty-One," *Transactions of the American Philological Association* 110 (1980): 255–61; J. Latacz, "Realitat und Imagination: Eine neue Lyrik-Theorie und Sapphos *phainetai moi kenos*-Lied," *Museum Helveticum* 42 (1985): 67–94.

NO EPITAPH

buds know themselves through hot and cold
(Bei Dao)

Because he grew up in the west he was used to the sound of the wind.
All day and all night, especially in spring, it streamed
through the world like hair.
Threw moonlight across the courtyard while he slept.
Forms chased forms, it slipped along the ledges, quieting itself.
Tap tap tapped the wooden blinds against the window like a blind man.

Who's there? his aunt called out in the swollen dawn.

The year he graduated the Cultural Revolution broke out.
Okay everything was a mess he says.
He joined the Red Guard.
Was sent to a nasturtium farm near the border of Russia
and there learned to live among people so different from himself
they stole his food. The first time it happened he was in the kitchen

rolling out dumpling wrappers with a bamboo flute for Spring Festival.

He and his colleagues were singing home songs and tasting late night air.
The kitchen at this hour was huge and different,
they worked
together in one small corner hearing their voices stop

....

before reaching very far. *The flying goose the wanderer*
how many days since I left home? (they sang) *the flying goose*

the wanderer both are gone one will return.

After returning to the dormitory to discover the theft he felt his chest
had been pried open and heart taken out.
Later he learned to bargain
for security with food filched from the kitchen.
Everyone was always hungry. Two oranges were worth
five nights of no stealing (usually). Meanwhile in the nation at large

there were occurrences.

An attempt was made to assassinate the Chairman of the government.
People seemed to be losing track of original meanings.
Many felt they had been deceived in something.
He wanted to face this in his mind, he read books all night
looking for the true practice. There were debates with others.
He developed a "problem of standpoint" as it was called

by the senior officer assigned to change his opinions

which did not change and so were renamed a "problem
of cognitive ability" by the officer, a kindly old-time intellectual.
No military tribunal was called.
Due to his deep depression during this period
romantic feelings were stirred in many local girls—so he found out
later. Being extremely short-sighted he failed to respond at the time.

....

They called him One Page Document.

Thinking back on this saddens him now. *Okay who is that man?* he asks.
Until his notebooks were confiscated he had written a lot of poetry.
He thought of poetry as bread to be shared by all.
But can a gentleman live in compromise. *Okay better draw back.*
He quit the Guard, moved south, went to work in an aeroplane factory.
Speaking of these times he hesitates. It was a search for ordinary life,

meantime very hard work.

Work unrolled its calendar of long same hours and roaring machinery.
He liked to sit in the cafeteria with his earplugs out
rubbing against the solid evidence
of people talking, people eating, people sitting silent.
He had a book open. *What's that you've got there poetry?*
Read us something! So he read *I wonder if I had not been born*

who would be drinking this cup of coffee?

They looked at him. *Caught up in foreign stuff* said one
and went back to her meal. He kept his eyes
on the book
and pretended to go on reading.
Every bone in me belongs to others,
what a sly thief! Open my cold heart's oven—nothing but a surprised lizard!

The cafeteria never had enough food.

....

He had taken to keeping provisions in his room and so encountered
an authority fiercer than any he had met so far,
the mice.
When he switched on the light they had just
vanished over the boards. Their toothmarks in his carrots.
Their famine feet flickering back and forth in the walls at night.

Their ice cries taking tiny stitches in his dreams.

One night he was awakened by a soft sound like bumps in wind.
A mouse had got into the flour bag.
Suddenly crazy with anger
he jumped from bed, grabbed the bag by its drawstring top,
began to beat it against the floor. Just as suddenly the fit left him.
He stood looking down at the bag then opened it. Inside a dead mouse

and flour dyed with mouse blood.

Okay I ate this bag of flour eventually otherwise I would be hungry.
Flowing back, backward from that night he sees
a change beginning.
He is suddenly tired and looks out the door.
Sycamore trees at dawn are big, unbandaging themselves.
At the factory he used to read late into the night, all night.

It made the others curious.

But mostly they had decided to let him be. During political discussions
he had ideas no one could follow, for example that they find
new names

for the prevailing party factions, known at that time
as Right Opportunistic Line and Left Opportunistic Line.
It sounds like a railway timetable he said and proposed instead

Denver Rio Grande and *The Nickel Plate Road*

(he was reading a book about American narrow-gauge railways)
but the chairwoman asked him to sit down.
How could they understand
that he was truly practicing.
But his braindog got lonely. So he set about teaching himself
some jokes and games, to drink and chat and go hunting in the mountains.

Only one thing he could not be enticed to do,

steal cocks. No matter how they ridiculed. Why? He smiles.
He will never tell me. Maybe I don't need to know this.
Anyway
just then a strange circumstance
allowed him to overpower them once and for all.
He remembers a cave immense and dark and eight people standing.

All sound had gone out.

Was there some trouble? An old worker died of appendicitis
on the night shift and the body could not be cremated
until certain disputes
between the hospital and the family were resolved.
Someone would have to watch the body, they stood in a small circle,
shadows straining away from them toward all high corners of the room.

He was as surprised as anyone to hear himself say he would do it.

What was it like? *Quiet* he says. Each night for a week
he kept company beside the empty arms of the dead.
Looking out the door we can see Venus rising.
Okay there she is.
Cold rushes in.
No need for men to chatter so.

Page of His

This is a song on the death and burial of one prince.

To utter it how strangely awful.

While the shining days are piled up.

He will have been perfect my beloved prince.

When spring came along the road under the pines

(the word for "pines" sounding like the word "to wait for a faraway person")

going up that road, glancing over the land.

When he was buried.

I know not where to go.

Pines touched by his sleeve's passing one cannot ask them

being but a tree, but still!

APPENDIX TO ORDINARY TIME

My mother died the autumn I was writing this. And *Now I have no one,* I thought. "Exposed on a high ledge in full light," says Virginia Woolf on one of her tingling days (March 1, 1937). I was turning over the pages of her diaries, still piled on my desk the day after the funeral, looking for comfort I suppose—why are these pages comforting? They led her, after all, to the River Ouse. Yet strong pleasure rises from every sentence. In reflecting on the death of her own father, she decided that forming such shocks into words and order was "the strongest pleasure known to me" (*Moments of Being* [London 1985], 81).

And whom do we have to thank for this pleasure but Time?

It grows dark as I write now, the clocks have been changed, night comes earlier—gathering like a garment. I see my mother, as she would have been at this hour alone in her house, gazing out on the cold lawns and turned earth of evening, high bleak grass going down to the lake. Or moving room by room through the house and the silverblue darkness filling around her, pooling, silencing. Did she think of me—somewhere, in some city, in lamplight, bending over books, or rising to put on my coat and go out? Did I pause, switch off the desklamp and stand, gazing out at the dusk, think I might call her. Not calling. Calling. Too late now. Under a different dark sky, the lake trickles on.

How vanished everyone is, Virginia Woolf wrote in letters to several people in 1941. And to Isaiah Berlin, *Please knock on my little grey door.* He did not knock; she died before. Here is a fragment from February of that year:

It is strange that the sun shd be shining; and the birds singing.
For here,

it is coal black: here in the little cave in which I sit.

Such was the complaint of the woman who had all her faculties

entire.

~~She did not not sufficiently. She had no grasp of~~

(Berg Collection of the New York Public Library)

Reading this, especially the crossed-out line, fills me with a sudden understanding. Crossouts are something you rarely see in published texts. They are like death: by a simple stroke—all is lost, yet still there. For death *although utterly unlike life* shares a skin with it. Death lines every moment of ordinary time. Death hides right inside every shining sentence we grasped and had no grasp of. Death is a fact. No more or less strange than that celebrated fact given by the very last sentence of her diaries (March 24, 1941):

L. is doing the rhododendrons.

Crossouts sustain me now. I search out and cherish them like old photographs of my mother in happier times. It may be a stage of grieving that will pass. It may be I'll never again think of sentences unshadowed in this way. It has changed me. Now I too am someone who knows marks.

Here is an epitaph for my mother I found on p. 19 of the Fitzwilliam Manuscript of Virginia Woolf's *Women and Fiction:*

such

abandon   ~~Obviously it is impossible, I thought, looking into those~~

ment   ~~foaming waters, to~~

such   ~~compare the living with the dead make any comparison~~

rapture   ~~compare them.~~

....

Margaret Carson

1913–1997

Eclipsis est pro dolore.

A NOTE ABOUT THE AUTHOR

Anne Carson lives in Canada.

....

A NOTE ON THE TYPE

This book was set in a typeface called Walbaum.

The original cutting of this face was made by Justus Erich Walbaum

(1768–1839) in Weimar in 1810. The type was revived by

the Monotype Corporation in 1934. Although the type that bears his

name may be classified as modern, numerous slight irregularities

in its cut give this face its humane manner.

Composed by NK Graphics, Keene, New Hampshire

Printed and bound by Quebecor Printing, Fairfield, Pennsylvania

Designed by Dorothy Schmiderer Baker